Carl Engel

The Literature of National Music

Carl Engel

The Literature of National Music

ISBN/EAN: 9783337084509

Printed in Europe, USA, Canada, Australia, Japan

Cover: Foto ©Thomas Meinert / pixelio.de

More available books at **www.hansebooks.com**

THE LITERATURE

OF

NATIONAL MUSIC

BY

CARL ENGEL.

LONDON:
NOVELLO, EWER & CO.

1879.

[All Rights reserved.]

PREFACE.

THE present essay is republished from *The Musical Times* (London: Novello, Ewer and Co.), where it appeared in the monthly numbers from July, 1878, to March, 1879. Some additions have been made in order to render it convenient as a book of reference.

I shall not apologise for its republication, since it is not likely to interest any but intelligent inquirers. These, I doubt not, are convinced that, just as painters, sculptors, and architects find it useful and highly interesting to pursue the investigations of their respective arts among nations in different stages of civilisation, musicians also should take a wider view of their art than they are too apt to do.

The greatest obstacle to information which the student of National Music is likely to encounter, is the difficulty in gaining access to many of the publications bearing on the subject. Every European country ought to possess in its National Library not only all the collections of its own national songs and tunes, but also those of other countries. Most of these publications are out of print, and there is no probability, except in some rare instances, of their being republished. They become daily more scarce, and soon it will be impossible to collect them together, even for a National Library.

Perhaps this little book may be of some assistance to the librarian as well as to the musician.

CARL ENGEL.

CONTENTS.

NATIONAL MUSIC...	1
NATIONAL SONGS...	6
POETRY	44
DANCE-TUNES	54
SACRED MUSIC ...	63
MUSICAL INSTRUMENTS ...	70
TREATISES	81
VARIOUS SOURCES	93
INDEX	103

NATIONAL MUSIC.

I PURPOSE to give some account of the books relating to National Music which have been published in different countries. Before entering upon this subject, I venture to submit to the consideration of the intelligent musician a few introductory remarks, which may perhaps be of assistance to him in his perusal of the following survey, in case he should not previously have given particular attention to National Music as a science. Indeed, there is reason to surmise that the subject is rather new to many musicians; at all events, the present essay cannot claim to "supply a long-felt want in literature." Still, whoever has obtained some insight into the rich treasures of popular songs and tunes, which have been hitherto but little explored, will probably be convinced that the study of National Music is sure to become gradually more appreciated by the earnest promoters of the art.

As regards the term National Music, it must be remembered that, taken in its widest sense, it designates any music which, being composed in the peculiar taste of the nation to which it appertains, appeals more powerfully than other music to the feelings of that nation, and is consequently pre-eminently cultivated in a certain country. In this sense, Haydn, Mozart, and Beethoven may be regarded as representatives of German National Music; Rossini, Bellini, and Donizetti of Italian National Music; Auber, Boïeldieu, and Hérold of French National Music. However, distinguished composers have developed their style in great measure by studying the works of previous masters of different countries. The peculiar characteristics of the music of the nation are therefore more strongly exhibited in the popular songs and dance-tunes traditionally preserved by the country-people and the lower classes of society, which form the great majority of a nation. These musical conceptions, generally simple and unpretending in construction, often retain their popularity for a long period, since the views and sentiments of the uneducated or simple-minded man are less subjected to external influences than are those of the educated or ambitious man. Thus may perhaps be explained the fact that we find among the rural population in some countries tunes still sung which are known to be above a century old. True, they have been somewhat altered in the course of time. It is surprising that their alteration is not very great, considering that they have been preserved traditionally from mouth to mouth, at least only so by the country-people who own them.

Now, it is with this kind of music, or with National Music in a more strict sense of the term, and not with the elaborate productions of distinguished composers, with which the reader is invited to occupy his attention. But, it may be asked, what is the advantage of carefully investigating such inartistic musical effusions? The reply is: The study of National Music is useful on account of the great originality of popular tunes. Professional musicians have many inducements to compose or perform music which they do not feel, while the untaught peasant will sing when his heart's emotions impel him to it. No wonder that his musical effusions, artless as they may be, should often be a truer expression of feelings than well-constructed productions of clever artists.

The study of National Music is useful on account of the great variety in the popular tunes. This variety is really astounding, almost every nation's music having its own peculiar stamp. Through a familiarity with the popular tunes of many countries, so very different from each other, our musical conception becomes enlarged, and we learn more clearly that the rules laid down for our guidance in art are by no means so infallible as they may appear at first sight, but that most of them can not unfrequently be disregarded with advantage.

The study of National Music is useful on account of the great beauty of many of the popular tunes. If the reader is acquainted with some of the most admired Scotch, Irish, or Welsh songs, he will probably testify to the exquisite beauty and impressiveness of the airs. He may be assured that all European nations possess such heartfelt melodies, only different in form and rhythmical expression; he will find this to be the case, if he is not deterred by their strange characteristics from familiarising himself with them thoroughly. The characteristics are, in many instances, so greatly at variance with those which distinguish our own popular music, that an intimacy with them is only gradually obtainable. Especially the tunes, or melodious phrases, of the Arabs, Hindus, Chinese, and several other extra-European nations, appear to us on first acquaintance almost as unintelligible as a language with which we are but very slightly acquainted. Howbeit, also these nations possess beautiful airs of popular songs. Their conceptions are perhaps all the more interesting to the student, since the airs are founded on successions of intervals, or scales, different from our own scales.

Again, the study of National Music is useful in an historical point of view, because it affords us an insight into the different stages of development of the art of music in different countries. Besides, popular ballads and other compositions are not unfrequently associated with important national events, by which they were called forth, or which they promoted.

The study of National Music is also useful in ethnological researches, as it gives us an insight into the inward man, reveals the character and temperament of different races, and the degree of affinity which exists between the different human families. Perhaps it would be more correct to consider a knowledge of it desirable in the pursuit of anthropology, which treats on the natural history of man, rather than of ethnology; for the latter science is only a branch of the former, and treats on the relations of the different varieties of mankind to each other. But it may well be doubted whether National Music will ever become of essential use in these sciences; certainly it cannot compare with languages in this respect. Music is too fugitive; the construction and mode of expression of its compositions are constantly subject to modifications. At any rate, this is the case in civilised nations. Among uncivilised nations not affected by European influence, any changes of this kind are much more gradual, and may scarcely be traceable during centuries. Besides, an exact knowledge of National Music is not sufficient for the purpose in question : an acute feeling for its beauties and various characteristics is equally requisite. But it is a rare coincidence when scientific men possess this acute feeling, which is, in fact, a musical talent, not attainable by study, though capable of development like other innate gifts. However, this question needs no further consideration here, since it does not immediately concern the musical student.

Likewise will it suffice merely to allude to the interest which popular songs possess for the philologist, on account of the languages and the dialects exhibited in poetry of different countries and different districts of a country. Moreover, the poetry is, as is well known, often of great beauty—indeed, not less so than the music; and deserves for this reason the attention of the artistic mind.

Now, should the previous statements have convinced the reflecting musician of the advantage of an acquaintance with National Music, he will perhaps be glad to know the proper sources for information, and the nearest way of access to them. Many of the printed collections of popular songs and tunes have been published in out-of-the-way places, in foreign countries, and have not become known through the usual channel of the book trade, for the obvious reason that they were only issued for the people to whom they belong, others not caring about them. It is often difficult to obtain a copy of such a publication; indeed, it requires almost a lifetime to hunt up the most important ones, and to collect them together. The collector must be prepared for frequent disappointments, occasioned by the promising titles of worthless compilations, which he is tempted to order from foreign countries. Just as is the case with other literary productions, the really valuable works have generally more modest titles than those which possess comparatively but little merit.

As the following survey is intended to save the student disappointment and time, by drawing his attention to the most important works, publications which are out of print or are otherwise not easily accessible will be noticed more fully than those which may be supposed to be known to many musicians. In order not to enlarge the survey to an inconvenient length, many publications which have no especial claim to consideration will be left unnoticed. The reader must therefore not expect to find an exhaustive list of works on the subject under discussion.

NATIONAL SONGS.

COLLECTIONS of national songs which contain merely notation of the airs, with the words, are generally the most desirable for the musical student. In many collections a pianoforte accompaniment has been added which is foreign to the original music and which obscures its characteristics. Pianoforte arrangements of airs, in which the words have been omitted, are generally the least useful, since it is seldom possible to ascertain from them how much is genuine, and to disentangle the original air from the interspersions and ornamentations of the arranger. The popular songs of most nations are usually sung by a single voice, or by a number of voices in unison; harmony is employed only in exceptional instances. When in a collection the tunes are faithfully rendered in notation, the student, by being supplied with an additional harmony, has only the disadvantage of possessing a more bulky and expensive book than he requires. Be this as it may, the pianoforte accompaniments of national songs are often far too elaborate, and anything but tasteful. If the song is to be accompanied, the harmony should, as a rule, be as unpretentious as possible; perhaps a few chords, such as the common chord, on the tonic, on the dominant and subdominant, occasionally struck and long sustained, will be found to answer the purpose best; although the peculiar modulations prevailing in the airs of certain nations require some unusual successions of chords, if they are to be harmonised at all.

In examining the collections, the student will probably soon become convinced that national songs are most effective without the usual attempts of professional musicians to dress them up to greater advantage. As it is, a harmonised national tune conveys not unfrequently a ludicrous impression, somewhat similar to that which might be conveyed by the sight of a peasant attired in a fashionable evening dress behaving awkwardly in a drawing-room party.

A published collection of national airs, containing genuine specimens from every country, is still an unaccomplished work. The largest collection of the kind which has hitherto appeared in print was compiled by Andreas Peter Berggreen, a professional musician in Copenhagen, and dates from the year 1855. It is entitled "Folke-Sange og Melodier," and consists of four volumes in oblong folio. A second edition, greatly enlarged, was published in the year 1862, and comprises ten volumes. The songs are with pianoforte accompaniments, and dance-tunes arranged for the pianoforte are interspersed; but it can hardly be said that the editor has been successful with his arrangements. The songs are almost exclusively from European nations; the collection is therefore far from sufficiently comprehensive for the study of national songs. As might perhaps be expected from the circumstance of the editor being a Dane, the Scandinavian airs comprise a large portion of the work, the first volume containing above two hundred Danish tunes harmonised. Another publication of the kind, but much smaller, is by O. L. B. Wolff, and appeared about the year 1840, by Simrock, in Bonn. It is entitled "Braga," and contains additional pianoforte accompaniments to the original airs, and German translations of the original poetry. Somewhat similar publications, such as "Bardale," edited by Baumstark and Waldbrühl (Leipzig), "Cent Chants populaires, par G. Fulgence" (Paris), "Orpheus," edited by Kayser (Hamburgh, 1853), are too insignificant to be useful for study. The same may be said of the English publications by Edward Jones, entitled "Lyric Airs" (London, 1804), and "Musical Curiosities" (London, 1811); likewise of Clementi's "Selection from the Melodies of different Nations;" and of the national tunes arranged for the pianoforte by W. Crotch, which form the first volume of his "Specimens of Various Styles of Music;" and others.

Let us now examine the collections restricted to the songs of single nations, in which we find more useful information. To begin with the Scandinavians (the Danes, Swedes,

Norwegians, Icelanders, and Faroe Islanders), who have proved themselves zealous collectors of their beautiful popular songs. As far back as in the year 1591 Sofrenson Vedel, a parson in Denmark, published a number of those famous Danish ballads called "Kämpeviser;" of which, in the year 1695, Peter Syv brought out a greatly enlarged edition. Especially noteworthy is a collection by Abrahamson, Nyerup, and Rahbek, entitled "Udvalgte Danske Viser fra Middelalderen" (Copenhagen, 1812; sm. 8vo, five vols.), which contains, in an appendix, a number of tunes in notation. A supplement to this important work was published by P. Rasmussen and R. Nyerup, in two volumes 8vo (Copenhagen, 1821).

Among the Swedish publications, the student ought to consult especially "Svenska Folk-Visor," by Geijer and Afzelius (Stockholm, 1846; 8vo, three vols.); "Svenska Fornsånger," by Arwidsson (Stockholm, 1834-42; 8vo, three vols.); "Svenska Vallvisor och Hornlåtar," by R. Dybeck (Stockholm, 1846; 8vo). The two last-named works have the notation of the airs without any attempts at improvement by unwarranted arrangements or additions; the work edited by Geijer and Afzelius has a pianoforte accompaniment to the airs, which was made by J. C. F. Haeffner, a German musician residing in Stockholm. There is also an interesting collection of Swedish songs and dance-tunes arranged with pianoforte accompaniments, by Ahlström and Boman (Stockholm, Hirsch, folio); and another, edited by A. G. Rosenberg, and entitled "160 Polskor, Visor och Danslekar uppteeknade i Södermanland, samt sattei för Pianoforte" (Stockholm, 1876; folio).

The most recommendable Norwegian collections are "Norske Folkviser" by M. B. Landstad (Christiania, 1853; 8vo), and "Gamle Norske Folkviser," by Sophus Bugge (Christiania, 1858; 8vo). Both of these works are carefully edited. Landstad is a Norwegian clergyman, and we are informed that his present collection of Norwegian minstrelsy was gathered from the lips of the people. It comprises 113 tunes, which are printed at the end of the volume of poetry. Sophus Bugge, a young student of antiquarian taste and knowledge, about the year 1856 visited the remote villages of Norway, at the expense of the Swedish Government, to collect all the metrical tales and traditions that still linger there. Perhaps it may interest some readers of a linguistic taste to be apprised of a little book with tunes which is entitled "Norske Viser og Stev i Folkesproget," and of which a second edition was published by Jorgen Moe (Christiania, 1848; sm. 8vo). The songs are in the dialect of the peasantry, which differs from the Danish language spoken by the educated classes in Norway. Furthermore, there requires to be noticed the "Norske Fjeldmelodier," arranged for the pianoforte by L. M. Lindeman, a learned musician in Christiania, and published in folio. This work contains 283 tunes, which the student may find useful if he has the patience to extricate them from the constant changes in harmony, imitations according to the rules of counterpoint, and other clever contrivances testifying to the editor's skill as a theorist.

Turning to the Slavonic races (the Russians, Poles, Czechs, Wendes, Serbes, &c.), we again meet with several very interesting publications. The Russians especially have not neglected to collect their fine songs and tunes. The most noteworthy Russian books of the kind are by the following editors: Michailow Tchulkow (St. Petersburg, 1770-88); Michailow Popow (St. Petersburg, 1792); Dmitriew (Moscow, 1796); Katalim (Moscow, 1810); Baikow (St. Petersburg, 1814); Shukowsky; Glasunow; Prince Zertülow. The first edition of the well-known collection of Russian popular songs with pianoforte accompaniment, by T. Pratch, was published in St. Petersburg in the year 1790, in one volume 8vo; a second edition, in two volumes 4to, appeared in 1806, and a third edition in 1815. It contains an introductory essay on the Russian national song, written by Lwow. There is also a noteworthy publication of ancient and modern Russian songs arranged for the pianoforte, and issued in three volumes 8vo, by Gerstenberg and Ditmar, in St. Petersburg. More recently, A. Kocipinski has brought out a collection of one hundred airs sung in the Ukraine and Podolia. This work, entitled "Pisni, Dumki, i Szumki Ruskoho," &c. (Kiev and

Kamenetz, 1861; royal 8vo), deserves especial attention. There is also an edition of it in folio, published in the same year, which contains a pianoforte accompaniment to the airs, but has only the first verse of the poetry to each air. In the pianoforte accompaniment the student will find vexatious examples as to how National Music ought not to be treated. The editor is probably a native of the district where the airs are at home; at any rate, his name indicates that he belongs to the Slavonic races, and, this being the case, it certainly appears strange that he should have so little caught the spirit of the music as to overload the accompaniment with all kinds of inappropriate passages and unmeaning modulations. It may perhaps seem unnecessary to the reader to have his attention drawn to bad arrangements; but if he examines the publications pointed out in the present survey, he will soon become convinced how important it is, in examining a collection of tunes, to discern at once what is genuine and what is spurious. My observations are intended to facilitate his labour. Other collections of national airs of Little-Russia are by Halahan, Lyssenko, &c.

The Russian language is so little cultivated in Western Europe, that but few English musicians are likely to be able to understand the poetry of the songs just noticed. There are, however, some German translations of Russian songs, with the original tunes, which may perhaps be more convenient to the English student of Slavonic music. Take, for instance, "Russische Volkslieder," by G. von Doppelmair (Leipzig: Breitkopf and Härtel; 4to), and "Die beliebtesten Russischen Volkslieder übersetzt von Grünbaum" (Berlin: Schlesinger; folio).

Having thought it necessary to protest against certain tasteless arrangements, it is to me a duty all the more pleasant to draw attention to the discernment evinced by Oskar Kolberg, in his "Piesni Ludu Polskiego" (Warsaw, 1857; 8vo), which contains 466 Polish airs of songs and dance-tunes. Only the melody is given with the words of the songs: deviations popular in certain districts of Poland are indicated with small notes. In the dance-tunes occasionally some harmony is admitted, precisely as the people are in the habit of introducing it. Moreover, the book is embellished with ten coloured plates representing Poles in their national costumes. Oskar Kolberg is a native of Poland, and studied music for some time in Berlin. On his return to Warsaw he made it one of his principal objects to investigate the National Music of his country. He also published 126 Polish airs with pianoforte accompaniments (Posen, 1842; folio). A collection of Polish songs, by A. Sowinski (Paris, 1830; folio), has a French translation printed together with the original words. Especially noteworthy are also the songs of the people in Cracow, published by Konopka (Cracow, 1840); and the songs of the White-Crobatians, Masovians, and Russinnians on the river Bug, published by K. W. Wojcicki (Warsaw, 1836; two vols.). Songs of the Polish inhabitants in Eastern Prussia have been published by J. J. Lipinski (Posen, 1842; sm. 8vo); Julius Roger (Breslau, 1863; 8vo); Hoffmann von Fallersleben (Cassel, 1865; 8vo).

The Wends are a Slavonic race living in some villages of Lusatia, in Germany. A comprehensive collection of their popular songs, edited by Haupt and Schmaler (Grimma, 1841; 4to, two vols.), contains 530 songs with the tunes. The words are in Wendish, with a German translation; and the interesting work is illustrated with coloured plates representing Wendish men and women in their picturesque costumes, and various objects illustrative of their manners and customs.

A curious instance, showing how even a distinguished musician may be deceived in hunting out national tunes if he has not made the subject his study, occurs in " Piesni Polskie i Ruskie Ludu Galicyjskiego," a collection of popular songs of the Polish and Russian people in Galicia, published by Venceslas Zaleski (Lemberg, 1833; 8vo, two vols.). The second volume contains 160 airs, with pianoforte accompaniments, by Charles Lipinski, the celebrated violinist. He was a native of Galicia; nevertheless he admits in his publication, No. 80 of the set of tunes, an air which is in construction and expression so different from those of his native country that he might have surmised that it could not be Galician, although he was not aware that it is the melody of "Nel cor più non mi sento," from the opera of "La Molinara," by Paisiello, on which Beethoven has composed beautiful variations, and which is known in England as the air of "Hope told a flatt'ring tale." Other Galician popular songs have been collected and published by Zegota Pauli (Lemberg, 1838, 1839).

The Czechs are the Slavonic inhabitants of Bohemia. A valuable collection of their songs, edited by K. J. Erben (Prague, 1862 and 1864; 8vo, two vols.), contains 811 tunes with the original words. An earlier publication, by Erben and Martinowsky (Prague, 1847; 4to), contains 300 songs with pianoforte accompaniments. Particularly interesting are the incorporated twenty old songs of the Hussites, which a friend of Erben committed to notation from the lips of an old minstrel, in the district of Budweis in Bohemia. These Hussite tunes are mostly in the minor key, but are more wild than sad. Other noteworthy publications of Bohemian National Music are by Rittersberg and Weber (Prague); Frantisek Martinec (Prague, 1856; oblong 8vo); J. Vashak (Prague, 1844); W. A. Swaboda (Prague, 1829; 8vo); F. L. Czelahowsky (Prague, 1822-27); J. W. Kamaryta (Prague, 1832). There are also two fine collections of Moravian songs, edited by Frantisek Sushil. The first of these (Brunn, 1840) has the poetry printed in 12mo, and the music, consisting of 480 tunes without any accompaniment, in oblong folio. The other contains, in one volume 8vo, 800 songs, with their tunes, and was published in Brunn in the year 1860.

In the charming Wallachian airs arranged for the pianoforte by J. A. Wachmann, a music director at Bucharest, we have an instructive example as to how such music ought to be treated if it is to be arranged at all. In the present instance the difficulty was the greater, since the peculiar succession of tones prevalent in the Wallachian melodies, with the frequent occurrence of the interval called the superfluous (or augmented) second, rather invites the arranger to some unwarrantable treatment. Wachmann has not been misled to extravagances; the genuine melody is always clearly prominent, and the accompaniment renders the peculiar rhythm which distinguishes many of the Wallachian tunes. There are in all sixty-two melodies thus issued by Wachmann, in four numbers (Vienna: Müller; folio), and the first number dates from about the middle of the present century. Wachmann states, in a short preface to the third number, that he has taken great care to retain the original characteristics of the music, that he has not allowed himself to add even a note of embellishment, and that his chief endeavour has been to transfer the music, as he often heard it performed by the perambulating musical bands in Wallachia, to the pianoforte as faithfully as possible. The members of these bands are frequently gipsies. Any musician acquainted with Roumanian music will probably admit that Wachmann has succeeded remarkably well.

It is impossible to bestow a similar commendation on the pianoforte arrangement of Servian tunes by Alois Kalauz (Vienna: Müller; folio, in two numbers); however, as many of the airs have the Servian poetry, with a German translation of the words, given with the notation, it is possible to recognise the original tunes, and to pick out the grain from the chaff. Kalauz gives in the second number some Bosnian tunes, which cannot fail to interest the student on account of their great originality. Another collection of Servian airs, edited by Cornelius Stankovitz, in Vienna, is entitled "Serbské Piesme," and contains thirty songs with pianoforte accompaniment, published in two books. It is, however, already out of print. Here may also be noticed the songs of the Slavonic inhabitants of Carniola, edited by Achazel and Korytho, under the title "Slovenske Pjesni Krajnskiga Naroda" (Laibach, 1839).

The reader is undoubtedly aware that the Baltic provinces of Russia are to a great extent inhabited by non-Slavonic races. The most interesting of these, musically regarded, are the Finns. A collection of their songs, entitled "Suomen Kansan Laulantoja Pianolla Soitettavia" (Helsingissa, 1849; oblong 8vo), is edited by Collan and A. Reinholm. The tunes are with a pianoforte accompaniment. Among them are some curious "Runo-songs," which are restricted to the compass of a fifth, and are noted down in 5-4 time. The book contains a representation of the "kantele," the old national musical instrument of the Finns. As the Finnish language is but little known in England, a short abstract of the contents of the instructive preface of this book may assist the student. The editors state that twenty pastoral songs of the Finns were published at Gottland, in the year 1831, and ten songs some years later, by Europaeus. A collection entitled "Kánteletar" is edited principally by Lönnrot, who is also a contributor to the present collection. The costume of the girl playing the "kantele," represented in the frontispiece of the present work, exhibits the old national dress of the Finnish women. There is also a German translation of Finnish Runo-songs, by G. H. von Schröter (Stuttgart, 1834; 8vo), which contains tunes.

Of the popular songs of the Lithuanians there are some German books which may assist the musical student unacquainted with the Lithuanian language. One of these is by L. J. Rhesa (Berlín, 1843; 8vo), and contains a German translation as well as the original words, with a number of tunes given in an appendix; the other is by G. H. F. Nesselmann (Berlin, 1853; 8vo), and likewise has tunes at the end of the volume. The songs of Lithuania are called "Dainos," and this name is also the title of the book by Rhesa.

Proceeding now to Hungary, a country which, it must be remembered, is inhabited by about half-a-dozen different races, we have to consider especially the music of the Magyars, because they are the principal and dominant race of Hungary, and it is their music which is generally meant by the term Hungarian National Music. There are several interesting collections published of the beautiful songs of the Magyars. Gabriel Mátray has especially distinguished himself as an editor of them. His "Magyar Népdalok" (Ofen, 1852; folio), and a supplement to the work (Pesth, 1858; folio), should be known to the student, and will probably be found all the more useful since a German metrical translation of the poetry is printed in juxtaposition to the original Hungarian words. There are certainly many English musicians who may be supposed to be able to read German, though probably but few who understand the Hungarian language. Gabriel Mátray is also the editor of a volume of ancient Hungarian songs, with the airs, dating from the sixteenth century, which was published at the request of the Hungarian Academy (Pesth, 1859; 4to). It contains an historical ballad, composed by Andras Farkas, in the year 1538; nineteen sacred songs, composed during the years 1538-52; a satirical song by Kristóf Ormpruzt, *anno* 1550; twenty-five historical and other songs, by Sebestyén Tinódi, a famous Hungarian bard, composed during the years 1541-53; and two songs made by the same bard in 1553 and 1554. The preface, written by G. Mátray, gives some account of the cultivation of music in Hungary during the sixteenth century, and especially of the musical notations as exhibited in the manuscripts of that period.

As another editor of interesting Hungarian collections of songs may be noticed Ignac Bognar (100 songs, Pesth, 1853; folio: 50 songs, Pesth, 1858; folio; &c.). J. Freichlinger, in Pesth, has published a set of Hungarian pastoral songs, with pianoforte accompaniment, under the title "Csikós dalai Zongorára." But we must not linger in Hungary, as we have still a long journey before us.

Let us next proceed to Turkey, a country in which the popular music partakes of an Oriental character, and in which musical instruments are in use which are almost identical with those of the Arabs and the Persians. No doubt in the principal towns of Turkey this is somewhat different, at least among the higher classes, whose taste has been more or less modified by the influence of European civilisation. At any rate, it is a well-known fact that the ladies in the harems at Constantinople not unfrequently have a pianoforte in their rooms, although they seldom achieve so much as to be able to play anything from notation. Some insight into the nature of their performance is afforded us by "Lyre Orientale," published in Constantinople in the year 1858. This is certainly one of the most extraordinary music-books ever printed. It contains Turkish songs, and several instrumental pieces, arranged for the pianoforte. The title-page, which is in French as well as in Turkish, informs us that they have been harmonised, by Mr. G. Guatelli, " Directeur de la Musique Impériale," assisted by Messrs. Arisdaguès Hohannessian and Gabriel Eramian, two Turkish "Professeurs de Musique" in Constantinople; and the work is dedicated to A.S.E. Nedjib Pacha, Gouverneur-général de la Musique de S.M.A. le Sultan." What strikes one at a first glance into these pianoforte arrangements is a frequent employment of a quick repetition of the same note, a method which Thalberg has employed to obtain a sustained though trembling sound. Perhaps the Turkish professors intended to imitate by this tremulousness the admired vibrating tones of their voices; for no doubt they are singers as well as pianists.

Another very remarkable book of Turkish music was published in Vienna about the year 1835, and contains fifty-nine songs of the Mewlewi Dervishes, with a pianoforte accompaniment written by the Abbé Maximilian Stadler. The Mewlewi Dervishes, who have their name from their founder, used to perform their sacred dances in a mosque at Tophané, a suburb of Constantinople. Herr von Hussard, secretary to the Austrian Legation in Constantinople, a great lover of music, often witnessed these dances, or "zikrs," as they are called, which are executed with the musical accompaniments of singing, playing on flutes, and beating of drums: and, with care and perseverance, he succeeded in faithfully rendering the songs in our notation. Having on his return to Vienna placed the manuscript in the hands of the Abbé Stadler, well known as a musician and as a friend of Mozart, Stadler wrote an accompaniment to the songs, contrived in his usual manner, which would probably have astonished the Dervishes, could they have heard it. At all events, however well acquainted pianoforte-players may be with the so-called "Alberti-bass" and "Murky-bass," so greatly favoured by the Abbé, to the Dervish it might very likely be puzzling. However, as the tunes are separately printed, with the original words and a German translation under them, it matters not greatly how the accompaniment is contrived. The title of the work is "Original-Chöre der Derwische Mewlewi" (Vienna: Pietro Mechetti; oblong folio). I regret that it would take too much space here to give a more detailed description of this curious book. Suffice it, for the right comprehension of the music, to point out that there is said to be a deep and mysterious signification in the sacred evolutions of those fanatics, in which a superior Dervish, seated in the centre, represents the sun, and those moving round him are stars of the planetary system. Also the words of their songs are asserted to have a deep meaning full of profound wisdom. In the German translation they appear rather bombastic and nonsensical; but it is perhaps difficult for an uninitiated European observer to fathom the depth of such Oriental lore.

As regards Greece, many collections of the popular songs of that country have been published in French or in German translations; but only a few of them contain airs in notation. Leopold Schefer has issued a supplement to the "Taschenbuch zum geselligen Vergnügen" (Leipzig, 1823; 12mo), which contains tunes of the modern Greeks; and there is an appendix of similar tunes in "Volksleben der Neugriechen," by D. H. Sanders (Mannheim, 1844; 8vo). Again, G. F. Weitzmann, in his short account of the music of the ancient Greeks (Berlin, 1855; 4to), gives forty popular melodies of the modern Greeks. Here also may attention be drawn to a little collection of new Greek songs edited by Gnéditch, a Russian gentleman (St. Petersburg, 1825). In the preface to this book are pointed out certain resemblances between the popular poetry of the modern Greeks and that of the Russians. Musicians are perhaps more interested in the ecclesiastic music of the Greek Church. On this subject a few statements shall presently be offered, since it appertains to national music, properly speaking.

The Greek songs recently published under the title "Trente Mélodies populaires de Grèce et d'Orient recueillis et harmonisées par L. A. Bourgault-Ducoudray" (Paris, 1876; folio), are especially noteworthy, inasmuch as they evidence discriminate appreciation of the duties of an editor of national airs. Of the thirty songs which the book contains, about half the number have been collected in Smyrna; the others are from Athens. The editor gives with each air an explanation of the peculiar scale on which it is founded; and he assures us, in the preface, that the original characteristics of the airs have been scrupulously preserved.

In Italy, the music-publisher B. Girard, of Naples, has earned the thanks of the lovers of National Music by bringing out his "Passatempi Musicali," which consists of a large set of Neapolitan and Sicilian airs of songs and dances, arranged for the pianoforte, and printed in folio. Another "Passatempi Musicali," issued by Rossi and Co., in Rome, comprises about thirty Roman tunes arranged for the pianoforte (folio). Perhaps more easily accessible to the student is "Collezione di Canzonette," &c., with a German translation of the Italian words, by G. W. Teschner (Berlin; oblong folio); or, "Alcuni Canti Populari Toscani," &c., edited by R. Lacy (London: Lonsdale; folio).

In Spain we meet with several collections of Boleros, Fandangos, and similar tunes, published by Martin in Madrid; as, for instance, "Las Castañuelas, coleccion de Bailes y Cantares Nacionales para Piano" (folio, two books). Several Spanish pianists and singers, such as M. S. Allu, Isidoro Hernandez, B. X. Miré, José Rogel, Carrafa, have had their transcriptions of, or rhapsodies on, Spanish national tunes brought out by Martin in Madrid. The Peninsular Melodies, compiled by G [eorge] L [loyd] (London, 1830; folio, two vols.), are genuine Spanish and Portuguese airs, to which poetry by English authors has been substituted for the original words.

In Portugal, F. D. Milcent has published a large volume of "Modinhas," as the national songs of that country are called. This publication, which is entitled "Jornal de Modinhas com acompanhamento de Cravo" (Lisbon; folio), dates probably from the end of the last century, when the harpsichord was still in use; for *cravo* signifies the harpsichord or clavicymbalum, which was also called gravicymbalum; hence probably the Portuguese *cravo*. Twelve Modinhas with their original words and an English translation, by Madame F. M., appeared in England under the title "Lusitanian Garland" (London: Ewer and Co.; folio).

Of the Basque people, who dwell in the north of Spain and the south-west of France, a collection of songs, with the airs, entitled "Eusculdun añcina añcinaco" &c. (San Sebastian, 1828; small folio), is edited by Francisco Iztueta, and contains a preface written in Spanish. There are also dance-tunes in this publication. It is now scarce; and this is likewise the case with a description of the dances of the Basques in Guipuzcoa, written in the Basque language by Don Juan Ignacio de Iztueta, and entitled "Guipuzcoaco dantza gogoangarrien," &c. (San Sebastian, 1824; 8vo). The Basque language being entirely different from any other European language, and known but to few persons besides those whose mother-tongue it is, the musical student will find it probably advisable to consult "Le Pays Basque" by Francisque-Michel (Paris, 1867; 8vo), which contains a whole chapter on music, and also about half-a-dozen tunes in notation. Moreover, respecting the Basques dwelling on the French side of the Pyrenees, he will find the desired information in "Chants populaires du Pays Basque, paroles et musiques originales, recueillis et publiées avec traduction française par J. D. J. Sallaberry" (Bayonne, 1870; royal 8vo), which contains, besides a great number of tunes, a French translation in juxtaposition to the original Basque poetry.

The French, as might be expected from their intelligence and antiquarian taste, have not neglected to investigate the popular legends, tales, and songs of their country. The object of the present survey does not demand a detailed account of the result of their researches. Suffice it to draw attention to the following publications: "Chants et Chansons populaires de la France; nouvelle édition illustrée" (Paris, 1848; royal 8vo, three vols.). "Chansons populaires des Provinces de France; notices par Champfleury; avec accompagnement de piano par J. B. Wekerlin" (Paris, 1860; royal 8vo). "Echos du Temps Passé," par J. B. Wekerlin (Paris, 1856-57; royal 8vo, two vols.). "Chants et Chansons des Provinces de l'Ouest, Poitou, Saintonge, Aunis et Angoumois, avec les airs originaux, recueillis et annotés par Jérome Bujeaud" (Niort, 1866; royal 8vo, two vols.). "Chansons et Airs populaires du Béarn, recueillis par

Frédéric Rivarès" (Pau, 1844; royal 8vo). "Poésies populaires de la Lorraine; publication de la Société d'Archéologie Lorraine" (Nancy, 1854; 8vo).

The collections confined to certain districts of France, of which more could be quoted did space permit, are generally the most valuable, since they give new information gathered from personal observation, songs with the tunes written down from the lips of the people, and explanations about the dialect and usages prevailing in the district; while the collections embracing specimens of songs of a whole country are usually compiled from those works, and supply only information obtained at second-hand. In support of this statement may be cited the interesting collection of the songs of Brittany published by Hersart de la Villemarqué, under the title "Barzaz-Breiz" (Paris, 1846; 8vo, two vols.). The edition here indicated is the fourth, greatly augmented, and provided with a French translation in addition to the original words. It must be remembered that the people of Brittany, or the French Bretagne, speak a language of their own, which is a Celtic dialect rather resembling the Welsh. However, the musical student, if he cares not for having the original language, may be referred to the English translation of "Barzaz-Breiz" by Tom Taylor (London, 1865; 4to), or to the German translation by Keller and Seckendorff (Tübingen, 1848; 8vo), although these reproductions contain only a small selection of the airs to be found in the comprehensive work of Villemarqué.

We must not leave France before having at least a cursory glance at the interesting French publications of songs of the olden time relating to our inquiry. The "Anthologie Françoise, ou Chansons Choisies depuis le 13ᵉ siècle jusqu'à présent" (Paris, 1765; 8vo, three vols.), deserves especial attention. Likewise "La Clef des Chansonniers, ou Recueil des Vaudevilles depuis cent ans et plus, notez et recueillis pour la première fois par J. B. C. Ballard" (Paris, 1717; sm. 8vo, two vols.); and "La Clé du Caveau à l'usage de tous les Chansonniers français, des Amateurs, Auteurs, Acteurs du Vaudeville, et de tous les Amis de la Chanson; par C * * * du Caveau Moderne" (Paris, 1811; oblong

12mo). This curious book, which contains nearly nine hundred tunes, might be compared to an English publication about a hundred years older, called "The Dancing Master." In the beginning of the present century there was still in Paris a musical and literary society, the members of which called themselves "Enfans de Caveau," because they had their meetings at a certain wine-room known as the Caveau.

Considering that the inhabitants of Switzerland consist of several races, we may expect to find with them songs in different languages. In the western cantons of Switzerland French is spoken; in Ticino, Italian; but about three-fourths of the population of Switzerland speak dialects of German, and as these constitute a large majority, it is chiefly their music to which we have to direct our attention. For this purpose may be especially recommended : "Sammlung von Schweizer-Kühreihen und Volksliedern" (Bern, 1818; oblong folio), which contains interesting introductory observations on the "Ranz de Vaches," by G. J. Kuhn and J. R. Wysz. This is the third edition of a successful publication; a fourth edition (Bern, 1826) contains, besides songs, several dance-tunes, and among these are two from the canton of Appenzell, which are given in notation for a violin, a dulcimer, and a bass, precisely as the collector heard them played by the country-people. A combination of these instruments is so rarely found in our scores that it may amuse the student to examine the pieces, which are by no means devoid of spirit and characteristic features. The "Recherches sur les Ranz des Vaches, ou sur les Chansons pastorales des Bergers de la Suisse, avec musique," by G. Tarenne (Paris, 1813; 8vo), contains a number of tunes as they are played on the alphorn in the different cantons of Switzerland. Furthermore, a noteworthy series of "Airs Suisses," with accompaniment of the guitar as well as the pianoforte, has been issued by A. Hegar in Basle.

The Germans have published more collections of national songs than any other nation. Here, again, must be borne in mind that, for the reason already stated, those collections which refer to a certain district of the country are generally the most instructive. It is rather difficult to contrive a satisfactory selection from a great number of publications, many of which are meritorious; to name them all here is out of the question, neither is it desirable. The following names of some of the editors, with an indication of the dates and the names of the places where their works appeared in print, may help to put the inquisitive student on the right track: Kretschmer und Zuccalmaglio (Berlin, 1838-40; 8vo, two vols.); Erk und Irmer (Leipzig, 1843; sm. 8vo); L. Erk, "Deutscher Liederhort" (Berlin, 1856; royal 8vo), Büsching und von der Hagen (Berlin, 1807; poetry, 12mo; music, oblong 8vo); F. Silcher (Tübingen, no date; oblong folio); Pocci, Richter und Scherer (Leipzig, no date; sm. 4to); Philipp Wackernagel, "Trösteinsamkeit" (Frankfort-on-Main, 1867; 12mo); &c.

As regards particular districts of Germany, there require to be noticed: "Schlesische Volkslieder," by Hoffmann von Fallersleben and E. Richter (Leipzig, 1842; 8vo). This judiciously edited collection of three hundred songs of the country-people in Silesia affords, in my opinion, a suggestive example as to how national songs ought to be published. The tunes are written down as they were gathered from the mouths of the singers, without any additions. The place where each tune was obtained is mentioned. Deviations in the tunes, or what may be called different readings, preferred in certain places, are indicated with small notes. The poetry likewise is carefully treated; and frequent references to other well-known collections—not only German, but also Scandinavian, Slavonic, French, &c., as regards certain characteristics of the songs—greatly enhance the value of the book for study. "Fränkische Volkslieder," by Franz Wilhelm Freiherrn von Ditfurth (Leipzig, 1855; 8vo, two vols.), consists of a large collection of songs, made in the part of Bavaria which constituted the ancient Franconia. The first volume contains 180 sacred songs; and the second and larger volume contains 400 secular songs. They are all noted down in two-part harmony; and the editor says that the people usually sing them in this way. "Oesterreichische Volkslieder," by Tschischka and Schottky (Pesth, 1844; sm. 8vo), is an instructive collection of the songs of the German population of Austria. In an appendix is given an account of the German dialect of the Austrian peasants, with a glossary. Likewise noteworthy are "Die Oesterreichischen Volksweisen," by Anton Ritter von Spaun (Wien, 1845; 8vo); and "Salzburgische Volkslieder," by Maria Vinzenz Süsz (Salzburg, 1865; 8vo). The last-named book possesses an additional interest from the circumstance of the tunes having been collected in and near to the birthplace of Mozart. Some of these songs may have served the great composer as his first initiatory lessons; at all events, it may be surmised, from his acute susceptibility for music, that the simple and impressive popular airs which he heard in his earliest childhood cannot have been without some influence upon his taste and development; and several melodies in his works could be pointed out which corroborate this surmise.

Songs of the Austrian province of Carinthia have been edited by Edmund Freiherr von Herbert (Klagenfurt: Edward Liegel; folio); of Styria, by Carl Fischer (Wien: Diabelli; oblong folio); of the Tyrol, by Paul Schonner (Wien: Diabelli; oblong folio). J. Moscheles is the editor of "The Tyrolese Melodies as sung by the family Rainer" (London: Willis; folio), in which may be seen examples of that peculiar kind of Tyrolese singing in falsetto, which they call *jodeln*, and which is much more effective in their mountains than in a drawing-room.

A little book of German tunes of bygone days, entitled "Lieder und Weisen vergangener Jahrhunderte," compiled by C. F. Becker (Leipzig, 1853; sm. 4to), which is easily obtainable, will provide the musician of an antiquarian turn of mind with some interesting specimens of German popular songs of the sixteenth, seventeenth, and eighteenth centuries. For ascertaining the date of origin and the authorship of a certain number of German popular songs which can thus be traced, the reader may be referred to "Unsere volksthümlichen Lieder," by Hoffmann von Fallersleben (Leipzig, 1869; 8vo). The Germans published as early as in the sixteenth century collections of their national songs, such as "Ein Ausbund guter alter und neuer Liedlein," by George Forster (Nürnberg, 1539), and "Hundert und fünfzehn guter und neuer Liedlein," by Hans Ott (Nürnberg, 1544): nay, it is recorded that Charlemagne, a thousand years ago, caused the popular songs of the Germans to be collected.

The Dutch also have several old song-books of the kind, as, for instance—Camphuysen: "Stichtelijke Rymen" (Amsterdam, 1647; 4to); Starter and Vredeman: "Friesche Lust-Hof" (Amsterdam, 1621; oblong 8vo); Prins: "Medenblicker Scharre-Zoodtje" (Medenblick, 1650; sm. oblong 8vo); Valerius: "Nederlandsche Gedenck-clanck" (Haerlem, 1626; 4to), &c. As these works are now scarce, the musician interested in examining the old Netherlandish tunes may be referred to "Oude Vlaemsche Liederen," by J. F. Willems (Ghent, 1848; royal 8vo), which contains 258 songs, most of them with the airs in notation. In this work is also given a list of the various collections of Flemish and Dutch tunes which have been published, or are known to be extant in manuscript. However, a better edited work is "Chants populaires des Flamands de France, recueillis et publiés avec les mélodies originales, une traduction française, et des notes," by E. de Coussemaker (Ghent, 1856; royal 8vo). Coussemaker is so well known as a learned and discerning musical author that the student will expect, as a matter of course, to find his compilation instructive. Here may also be noticed a recent publication of some songs with their airs, historically interesting, entitled "Twaalf Geuzeliedjes uit de Geusen Liedenboecxkens van 1588 en later, met de oorspronkelijke wijzen waarop ze in den Spaanschen tijd gezongen werden; voor zang en klavier bewerkt en wortelijk toegelicht door Dr. A. D. Loman" (Amsterdam, 1872; royal 8vo).

The Walloons in Belgium speak a curious French dialect. A collection of their songs, with a supplement containing thirty-six airs in notation, is entitled "Choix de Chansons et Poésies Wallonnes, Pays de Liége, par MM. B *** et D ***" (Liége, 1844; 8vo).

We now arrive at the British Isles, where, especially in Scotland, we meet with numerous printed collections. Indeed, the Scotch can boast of possessing nearly as many publications of the kind as the French or the Germans; but whether their tunes are as judiciously edited is another question. A considerable number of them are arranged for the pianoforte with the omission of the words of the songs, and with the introduction of embellishments, brilliant passages, and variations. However, with these we have not to concern ourselves in our present inquiry. The following certainly deserve attention:—

"A Collection of Original Scotch-Tunes (full of the Highland Humours) for the Violin: Being the first of this kind yet Printed: most of them being in the compass of the Flute. London: Printed by William Pearson, in Red-Cross Alley in Jewin-street, for Henry Playford, at his shop in the Temple-Change, Fleet-street. 1700" (oblong 4to). Henry Playford was the second son of the well-known music publisher John Playford. The book, which contains thirty-nine tunes, is interesting inasmuch as it represents the oldest published collection of Scotch national tunes properly so termed.

"Orpheus Caledonius; or, a Collection of the best Scotch Songs, set to Musick by W. Thomson (London). Engrav'd and printed for the Author, at his house in Leicester Fields" (folio). This publication bears no date, but the editor entered it at Stationers' Hall on the 5th of January, 1725. It contains fifty songs, preceded by a dedication to the Princess of Wales (afterwards Queen Wilhelmina-Caroline), and followed by a notation of the same songs for the flute. In the index Thomson has marked seven songs with asterisks, and he says "the songs mark'd thus were composed by David Rezzio" (sic). They are "The Lass of Patie's Mill," "Bessie Bell," "The Bush aboon Traquair," "The Bonnie Boatman," "An' thou were my ain thing," "Auld Rob Morris," and "Down the burn, Davie." Mention is made of W. Thomson in Burney's "History of Music" (vol. iv., p. 647) and in Hawkins's "History of Music" (vol. iv., p. 7). Hawkins evidently mistook the second edition of this work for the first. The second edition, which is in two volumes, octavo, was published in the year 1733, and has not the asterisks referring to David Rizzio, the musician of Queen Mary Stuart.

"The Scots' Musical Museum; consisting of upwards of six hundred songs, with proper basses for the pianoforte;

originally published by James Johnson, and now accompanied with copious notes and illustrations of the Lyric Poetry and Music of Scotland, by the late William Stenhouse. New edition." (Edinburgh, 1853; 8vo, four vols. The first edition (London, 1787-1803) is in six volumes, 8vo. An edition with notes and illustrations of the lyric poetry of Scotland, by W. Stenhouse, and with additional illustrations by David Laing, was published in Edinburgh in the year 1839, and is likewise in six volumes 8vo. The introduction to the present edition contains the titles and description of a large number of published collections of Scotch airs. There is also a list of ninety-seven published collections and eight manuscripts in the introduction to "The Dance Music of Scotland," arranged and edited by J. T. Surrenne: second edition (Edinburgh: Wood and Co., 1852; royal 8vo).

"Ancient Scottish Melodies, from a manuscript of the reign of King James VI.; with an introductory enquiry illustrative of the history of the Music of Scotland," by William Dauney (Edinburgh, 1838; 4to).

"The Songs of Scotland, adapted to their appropriate melodies, arranged, with pianoforte accompaniments, by G. F. Graham, T. M. Mudie, J. T. Surrenne, H. E. Dibdin, Finlay Dun, &c.; illustrated with historical, biographical, and critical notices, by G. F. Graham" (Edinburgh: Wood and Co., 1856; royal 8vo, three vols.). It is indeed difficult to praise the pianoforte accompaniments in this publication, however much one may be disposed to judge them leniently; nevertheless, as the beautiful Scotch tunes are preserved intact, or have at any rate only occasionally been slightly tampered with, the student will find this publication useful for his purpose, especially on account of the annotations.

"The Songs of Scotland prior to Burns, with the Tunes," edited by Robert Chambers (Edinburgh, 1862; small 8vo). A carefully compiled and very interesting little book.

"The Jacobite Relics of Scotland; being the Songs, Airs, and Legends of the Adherents to the House of Stuart," collected and illustrated by James Hoggs (Edinburgh, 1819-21; 8vo, two vols.).

"Scottish Songs, with the Music," by Joseph Ritson (London, 1794; 12mo, two vols.); a second edition (Glasgow, 1869; 8vo, two vols.). The work contains an historical essay on Scotch songs.

"Ancient Scottish Ballads, recovered from Tradition, and never before published; with Notes, and an Appendix containing the Airs," by G. R. Kinloch (Edinburgh, 1827; 8vo).

There is a large publication of "Scottish Airs and Songs," by George Thomson (London, 1793-1841; folio, six vols.), who engaged Pleyel, Kozeluch, Haydn, Beethoven, Hummel, and Weber, to write pianoforte accompaniments to the melodies.

As regards the beautiful Irish airs, it may suffice to notice the following publications:—

"A General Collection of the Ancient Irish Music; containing a variety of admired Airs never before published, and also the compositions of Conolan and Carolan," by Edward Bunting (London, 1796; folio).

"A General Collection of the Ancient Music of Ireland, arranged for the Pianoforte; some of the most admired Melodies are adapted for the Voice, to poetry chiefly translated from the original Irish songs by Thomas Campbell, Esq., and other eminent poets; to which is prefaced a Historical and Critical Dissertation on the Egyptian, British, and Irish Harp," by Edward Bunting (London, 1809; folio, vol. i.). Only one volume has been published.

"The Ancient Music of Ireland, arranged for the Pianoforte: to which is prefixed a Dissertation on the Irish Harps and Harpers, including an account of the Old Melodies of Ireland;" by Edward Bunting (Dublin, 1840; 4to). In the preface, E. Bunting remarks that before the year 1796, when he published his first collection, "there had been but three attempts of this nature—one by Burke Thumoth, in 1720; another by Neill, of Christ Churchyard, soon after; and a third by Carolan's son, patronised by Dean Delany, about 1747."

"A Favourite Collection of Irish Melodies, the original and genuine compositions of Carolan, the celebrated Irish

Bard; arranged for the pianoforte, violin, or German flute; dedicated to the Irish Harp Society of Belfast" (Dublin, no date; folio).

"Historical Memoirs of the Irish Bards, interspersed with anecdotes of, and occasional observations on, the Music of Ireland; also an historical and descriptive account of the musical instruments of the Ancient Irish; and an Appendix containing several biographical and other papers, with select Irish Melodies," by Joseph C. Walker (London, 1786; 4to).

"A Selection of Irish Melodies; with symphonies and accompaniments by Sir John Stevenson, Mus. Doc., and characteristic words by Thomas Moore, Esq." (London: J. Power, 1807-34; ten parts, folio). There have subsequently been brought out some smaller editions of this work. Moore's fine poetry adapted to Irish airs has much contributed to make the Irish national music more widely known among the educated classes in different countries. The "symphonies and accompaniments" in the work, while containing much which is hardly desirable, leave much to be desired.

"The Petrie Collection of the Ancient Music of Ireland arranged for the pianoforte; edited by George Petrie, under the superintendence of the Society for the Preservation and Publication of the Melodies of Ireland" (Dublin: Gill, 1855; folio, vol. i.). Of this work the first volume only has been issued. It is rather diffuse, being overburdened with prolix introductory remarks and annotations; and the pianoforte arrangement is too elaborate to be in character with the tunes; otherwise the work is interesting.

Respecting the songs of Wales, there requires to be noticed first a curious publication which claims to be the earliest printed collection of Welsh tunes. I shall insert here its whole title, as I have done with some of the Irish books, because its character and purpose are therein so fully set forth, that it obviates the necessity of any further explanation. It is—

"Antient British Music; or a Collection of Tunes, never before published, which are retained by the Cambro-Britons, more particularly in North-Wales, and supposed by the learned to be the remains of the music of the antient Druids, so much famed in Roman history; Part I. containing twenty-four Airs set for the harp, harpsichord, violin, and all within the compass of the German flute, and figured for a thorough-bass. To which is prefixed an historical account of the rise and progress of Music among the Antient Britons; wherein the errors of Dr. Powel and his editor, Mr. Wynne, on that subject, in their history of Wales, are pointed out and confuted; and the whole set in its true and proper light. London: printed for and sold by the Compilers, John Parry, at his House in Jermyn Street, near St. James's Market; and Evan Williams, at Mr. Mickleborough's, in New Bond Street, near Union Street; and are to be had at the Music Shops. MDCCXLII." (sm. folio). Only the first part appears to have been published.

The following works ought likewise to be consulted by the student:—

"British Harmony; being a Collection of Antient Welsh airs, the traditional remains of those originally sung by the Bards of Wales; carefully compiled, and now first published with some additional variations, by John Parry; inscribed with all due esteem and gratitude to Sir Watkin Williams Wynn, Bart." (London: Hodgson, 1781; folio). This work, which contains forty-two airs arranged for the harpsichord, without the words of the songs, antecedes the publications by Edward Jones, who has adopted a similar plan in his arrangements with variations.

"Musical and Poetical Relics of the Welsh Bards, preserved by Tradition and Authentic Manuscripts from very remote antiquity, never before published. To the Bardic tunes are added variations for the harp, harpsichord, violin, or flute, with a select collection of the Pennillion, and Englynion, or epigrammatic stanzas, poetical blossoms, and pastoral songs of Wales, with English translations. Likewise a General History of the Bards and Druids from the earliest period to the present time, with an account of their music and poetry; to which is prefixed a copious dissertation on the musical instruments of the Aboriginal Britons. A new edition doubly augmented and improved, by Edward

Jones" (London, 1794; folio). Respecting the first edition (London, 1784; folio), Edward Jones, "Bard of His Royal Highness the Prince of Wales," observes, p. 123, "A few years ago I published a similar work; but, having since collected very important and more considerable documents on the subject, I thought it more judicious, instead of giving an additional volume, to blend the chief matter of the former publication with the present."

"The Bardic Museum; or primitive British Literature, and other admirable Rarities, forming the second volume of the Musical, Poetical, and Historical Relicks of the Welsh Bards and Druids; drawn from authentic documents of remote antiquity, with great pains now rescued from oblivion, and never before published; containing the Bardic Triads, Historic Odes, Eulogies, Songs, Elegies, Memorials of the Tombs of the Warriors of King Arthur and his Knights, Regalias, the wonders of Wales, *et cætera*, with English translations and historic illustrations. Likewise the Ancient War-tunes of the Bards. To these national melodies are added new basses, with Variations for the harp or harpsichord, violin or flute. Dedicated by permission to His Royal Highness the Prince of Wales, by Edward Jones, Bard to the Prince" (London, 1802; folio).

"A Selection of Welsh Melodies with Symphonies and Accompaniments, by John Parry; and Characteristic Words, by Mrs. Hemans" (London: J. Power, 1821; folio, two vols.). The first volume appeared some years earlier than the date here given, and was republished for the present edition, newly arranged, and with the poetry expressly written for it by Mrs. Hemans. It appears that the publisher, J. Power, instigated by the success of the Irish Melodies by Moore and Stevenson, to which also Sir Henry Bishop supplied some accompaniments, resorted to a similar expedient with the present Welsh Melodies, to only the first volume of which, however, it was extended. Perhaps more noteworthy to musicians is John Parry's statement in the preface: " I have purposely avoided all extraneous modulations and chromatic passages, that the accompaniments may be performed on the harp as well as on the pianoforte. I was strongly urged so to do, and requested to render the arrangement as simple and familiar as I possibly could, so that the melodies might not lose any of their character, or be disfigured by gaudy trappings."

"Ancient National Airs of Gwent and Morganwg; being a collection of original Welsh melodies hitherto unpublished, which obtained the prize at the Eisteddvod, held in celebration of the fifth anniversary of the Abergavenny Cymreigyddion, October, 1838, to which are added the words usually sung thereto. Collected and arranged for the harp or pianoforte, by M. Jane Williams, of Aberpergwm" (Llandovery, 1844; folio). Most of the tunes in the preceding publications were evidently collected in the northern and central districts of Wales. The melodies contained in the present volume, Miss Williams says, " have been collected among the peasantry of the districts of Gwent and Morganwg, especially in the Vale of Neath, one of the most romantic and secluded parts of the Principality of Wales, where the inhabitants retain much of their ancient pastoral and simple character, and the songs which suited the peaceful avocations of their forefathers are still to be heard in the farmhouse and the cottage. . . . In printing the present volume the collector disclaims all feelings of musical or literary ambition. The songs are given as she obtained them, in their wild and original state; no embellishments of the melody have been attempted, and the accompanying words are those sung to the airs." Considering how seldom even professional musicians have succeeded in writing appropriate pianoforte accompaniments to national airs, the shortcomings in the present arrangements may be easily excused, especially as we are told that the more important task of rendering a faithful notation of the tunes has been carefully attended to. Several of the tunes are remarkably beautiful.

" Y Caniedydd Cymreig; the Cambrian minstrel; being a collection of the melodies of Cambria, with original words in English and Welsh, together with several original airs," by John Thomas [Jeuan Ddu] (Merthyr Tydvil, 1845; 4to).
" Pencerdd; Gems of Welsh Melody; a selection of popular Welsh songs, with English and Welsh words; specimens of

Pennillion Singing, after the manner of North Wales; and Welsh national airs, ancient and modern, set in a familiar manner for the pianoforte or harp, with symphonies and accompaniments," by John Owen [Owain Alaw] (Ruthin, 1860; folio).

Here may also be noticed "The Mona Melodies; a collection of ancient and original airs of the Isle of Man, arranged for the voice with a pianoforte accompaniment by an Amateur; the words by Mr. J. B," edited by C. St. George (London: Mitchell, 1820; folio). The editor states in a preface that the melodies are genuine, but that "the words adapted to them are entirely new, as the subjects of the Manx ballads were not esteemed to be of sufficient general interest to warrant their translation," which is to be regretted.

It seems rather singular that England should not possess any printed collection of its national songs with the airs as they are sung at the present day; while almost every other European nation possesses several comprehensive works of this kind. One or two small publications such as the "Cheshire Melodies; provincial airs of Cheshire," by Edward Jones (London, about the year 1803), and "A selection of the most popular Melodies of the Tyne and the Wear, consisting of twenty-four original airs peculiar to the counties of Durham and Northumberland," published by Robert Topliff (London; folio), are too insignificant to supply the desideratum. Besides, they are too old to serve for illustrating the English national songs of the present time. Some musical inquirers have expressed the opinion that the country-people in England are not in the habit of singing while at their work in the fields, or when towards evening they are returning to their homes; and that those social gatherings during the long winter evenings, in which the Germans and other continental nations delight in singing their favourite songs, are unknown to the English rustics. However, this opinion would probably be found to be only partially correct if search were made in the proper places. Large towns are not the nurseries for the growth and preservation of national songs; and the circumstance of

England possessing many large towns may be the chief cause of the apparent dearth of such songs in this country. Still, there are in some of the shires rather isolated districts, in which the exertions of a really musical collector would probably be not entirely resultless. We have indications of this in several of the descriptions of English counties which have been published during recent years, and in which some tunes of the country-people have been given, with explanations of the peculiar manner in which they are sung on certain occasions. Likewise, several collections of popular poetry relating to different English counties, which have appeared in print since about the middle of the present century, as, for instance, "The Popular Rhymes, &c., of the county of Berwick," by G. Henderson (Newcastle-on-Tyne, 1856; 8vo); "Ballads and Songs of Lancashire," by J. Harland (London, 1865; 8vo), &c., suggest that there must be, belonging to the ditties, airs which have never been written down, and are only orally preserved by the people. We have seen that Miss Williams succeeded in bringing out a number of remarkably fine airs, hitherto unknown but to the villagers in the south of Wales, from whose singing she committed them to paper. The same might perhaps be accomplished in central and eastern England; and if the airs, as appears very likely, should prove less beautiful than those of Wales, they might be in every other respect equally interesting.

Of songs which were popular in former centuries, England possesses, as is well known, several collections of considerable comprehensiveness. As they may be supposed to exist in the libraries of many English musicians, I shall not try the patience of the reader by enlarging upon them. Suffice it to point out two or three by way of example.

"The Dancing Master," a collection of dance-tunes, has already been alluded to. Its first edition was published by John Playford, in London, in the year 1651. Many of the tunes which it contains are airs of popular songs of the time when the book was brought out.

"Wit and Mirth: or Pills to purge Melancholy; being a collection of the best Merry Ballads and Songs, old and new;

fitted to all humours, having each their proper tune for either voice or instrument; most of the songs being new set," by Thomas D'Urfey (London, 1719; 12mo, six vols.). An exact reprint of this work was published by Chatto and Windus, London, 1872. Not all the tunes which it contains are English, many are Scotch, others Irish, &c. Moreover, the original tunes are not unfrequently distorted to adapt them to the poetry written to them by D'Urfey.

"A Select Collection of English Songs," by Joseph Ritson (London, 1783; 8vo, three vols.); with an "Historical Essay on the Origin and Progress of National Song." The third volume contains the musical notation of the airs. There is also a second edition with additional songs and occasional notes by Thomas Park (London, 1813; 8vo, three vols.). However, the great majority of the airs printed in Ritson's "English Songs" can evidently not be regarded as national airs in a strict sense of the term, although the tunes may have been for some time in popular favour. The same remark applies to the airs in almost all the English collections of old songs. The difference between a national song (German, *Volkslied*) and a merely popular song (German, *Volksthümliches Lied*) is not always distinctly observed by the English musicians, and the two terms are often used indiscriminately.

"Musical Illustrations of Bishop Percy's Reliques of Ancient English Poetry; a collection of old ballad tunes, &c., chiefly from rare MSS. and early printed books; deciphered from the obsolete notation, and harmonised and arranged according to modern usage," by Edward F. Rimbault (London: Cramer, Beale and Co., 1850; royal 8vo).

"Popular Music of the Olden Time; a collection of ancient songs, ballads, and dance tunes, illustrative of the National Music of England. With short introductions to the different reigns, and notices of the airs from writers of the sixteenth and seventeenth centuries; also a short account of the Minstrels," by W. Chappell. The whole of the airs harmonised by G. A. Macfarren (London: Cramer, Beale, and Chappell, no date; royal 8vo, two vols.).

If I introduce here a tune, the patient reader will perhaps

surmise that I do it with the intention of somewhat relieving the unavoidable monotony of a long survey. I candidly admit that I should be glad if thereby I could render the survey more entertaining. This is, however, not my only reason for inserting the tune; if it were, should I choose the air of "God save the Queen," which every English musician may be supposed to know by heart, and most unmusical Englishmen too? Now, I hope the reader will not alarm himself with the idea that he must prepare himself for a discussion on the origin of the air of "God save the Queen." Unless some newly discovered and startling evidence could be advanced, the discussion would probably be as unprofitable as the usual investigations respecting the authorship of the Letters of Junius, or the real name of the mysterious W. H. to whom Shakespeare's Sonnets are dedicated. Every one who takes an interest in the matter knows that Richard Clarke, the author of "An Account of the National Anthem" (London, 1822; 8vo), assigns the tune to John Bull; and that others have pointed to Purcell, to Handel, nay, even to Lully in France, until Henry Carey's claim became fairly acknowledged. But it may interest the reader to learn a few facts respecting the adoption of the tune on the Continent, which, as far as I am aware, have not been noticed in any of the discussions and disputes on the origin of the famous song. It is in itself interesting to trace the introduction of a national air into a foreign country where it has taken root, and blossoms like a tree transplanted into a new soil; and the interest in tracing its growth is, of course, the greater the more highly the air is appreciated in its native country.

The earliest notation of the tune in question printed on the Continent occurs, as far as I am aware, in a song-book for Freemasons, published in Holland. The book contains songs in French and in Dutch, and is entitled "La Lire Maçonne, ou Recueil de Chansons des Franc-Maçons; revu, corrigé, mis dans un nouvel ordre, et augmenté de quantité de Chansons qui n'avoient point encore paru; par les frères De Vignoles et Du Bois. Avec les Airs Notés, mis sur la bonne Clef, tant pour le Chant que pour le Violon et la Flûte. Nouvelle Edition" (A la Haye: Van Laak, 1766; sm. 8vo).

In this book the tune is given to a Dutch poem entitled *D'Ongeveindsheid* ("Sincerity"), on page 166. According to an indication in the index the same song occurs also in the first edition of the work, which appeared three years previously to the present one; the tune was therefore printed in the year 1763. Under the Dutch heading are the words, "*Stem*, God seav' great George our King," which, to judge from the odd spelling of *save*, was evidently written by a foreigner unacquainted with the English language. The notation is as follows:—

It will be observed that this notation has already the triplet in the last bar but one, which, by filling up the step of a fifth, recorded to have been at first in the melody thus,

renders the singing easier. It must be borne in mind that this air is intended pre-eminently for all faithful subjects, be they musical or not; and, in order to be effectively sung in a grand unison, its steps of intervals require to be as convenient for the uncultivated voice as possible. It is interesting to see how the untutored people have unpremeditatedly smoothed over the original wide steps.

The air occurs also in an old Dutch collection of dance-tunes, which is perhaps of an earlier date than the first edition of the Freemasons' song-book. The collection alluded to is published in six small oblong octavo volumes, the first of which is entitled "De Nieuwe Hollandsche Schouwburg, zynde een Verzameling van verscheyden vrolyke en serieuse Danssen, nevens enige van de nieuwste *Zang Airen*, die voor de Viool, Dwarsfluyt, en anderen Instrumenten gebruykt kunnen worden; Eerste Deel; te Amsterdam, by Johannes Smit, boek en muziek verkoper op de Fluweele Burgwal by de Halsteeg." The fifth volume professes to contain only dance-tunes. Its title is "De Nieuwe Hollandsche Schouwburg, zynde een Verzameling van verscheyden vrolyke en serieuse Danssen, Menuetten, &c." There is no date of publication to the collection; however, to judge from the notation of the tune in question, which is printed in the fifth volume, and is headed " *God bles* (sic) *the King*," it is probably a very early importation from England. The notation is as follows:—

I am not aware that it was ever called in England "God bless the King;" but English musicians will probably be better informed about this, and may perhaps even be able to determine from the peculiar heading the age of the Dutch notation. That the Dutch should have used the air as a dance-tune is not surprising, considering that they had, as the title of the present collection intimates, serious dances. Nay, it is recorded that in olden time they danced, or shuffled about, to sacred tunes. The French, about the end of the sixteenth century, danced to psalm-tunes. The favourite dance-tune of King Charles IX. was the melody of Psalm cxxix: "Many a time have they afflicted me from my youth; yet they have not prevailed against me." It is therefore not so singular as it may appear that in the eighteenth century the Dutch should have used the English National Anthem as a dance-tune.

In the year 1790, Heinrich Harries, a clergyman in Schleswig, made a free translation into German of the English hymn of "God save the King," retaining the original air. The version was intended for the celebration of the birthday of King Christian of Denmark. From this hymn

Balthasar Gerhard Schumacher, a native of Holstein, and a Doctor of Law, constructed, in the year 1793, the hymn for Prussia, commencing "Heil dir im Siegerkranz!" ("Hail to thee in victor's wreath!") and thus the famous English air became naturalised in Germany. According to Hoffmann von Fallersleben ("Unsere Volksthümlichen Lieder," Leipzig, 1869, page 182) the second verse of the Prussian hymn—

Nicht Ross' und Reisige	Not horse and rider bold
Sichern die stolze Höh'	The lofty height may hold
Wo Fürsten stehn;	Where princes stand:
Liebe des Vaterlands,	Love of the fatherland,
Liebe des freien Manns	Love of the patriot band,
Gründet den Herrscherthron	Our royal throne shall keep
Wie Fels im Meer.	As sea-girt rock.

has often been objected to, and was actually suppressed on various solemn occasions, even as recently as in the year 1863, in many places. This, he says, induced a certain public singer of celebrity to substitute for its first word *Nicht* the word *Nur*, and to sing the obnoxious verse thus :—

Nur Ross' nur Reisige	True! horse and rider bold
Sichern die stolze Höh'	Alone the height may hold
Wo Fürsten stehn;	Where princes stand:
Liebe des Vaterlands,	Love of the fatherland,
Liebe des Burgermanns	Love of the patriot band,
Thun es allein nicht mehr	Is nought—an empty word,
Ohne das Heer.	But for the sword.

However, at the present day, every patriotic German may sing the proper verse from the bottom of his heart.

After this digression, which is perhaps longer than many readers care for, it is time to resume our survey. There are still the collections of songs of extra-European nations to be enumerated. This task will soon be accomplished, since there are comparatively but few publications of the kind worthy of consideration. The specimens of airs given in some treatises, which will later be mentioned, are the most reliable, and are certainly worthy of careful perusal. For instance, useful specimens of songs of the Arabs are given in an elaborate essay on the musical system of the Arabs, written by G. A. Villoteau, and printed in "Description de l'Egypt." Villoteau was a member of the scientific expedition which accompanied Napoleon Bonaparte to Egypt, in

the year 1798. As regards separate collections, the student ought to make himself acquainted with the following ones :—
"The Oriental Miscellany; being a collection of the most favourite Airs of Hindustan, compiled and adapted for the Harpsichord, &c.," by William Hamilton Bird (Calcutta: printed by Joseph Cooper, 1789; folio). This interesting publication, which is scarce, contains thirty tunes, preceded by a short introduction in which the editor explains the characteristics of the different kinds of songs of Hindustan. To some of the tunes the editor has added variations of his own composition; nevertheless, the work deserves the special attention of the collector of Hindu music. Similar but less important collections are "Hindoostanee Songs dedicated to Mrs. Bristow," by C. Trinks, organist of St. John's Church (Calcutta; folio); contains fifteen tunes. "Twelve Original Hindoostanee Airs, compiled and harmonised" by T. G. Williamson (London, about 1797; folio). "Second Collection of Twelve Original Hindoostanee Airs, compiled and harmonised" by T. G. Williamson (London, 1798; folio). "Twelve Hindoo Airs with English words adapted to them" (London: Birchall; folio), &c.

"The Hindustani Choral Book, or Swar Sangrah; containing the Tunes of those Hymns in the Gít Sangrah which are in Native Metres;" compiled by John Parsons (Benares: printed and published by E. J. Lazarus and Co., 1861; 8vo). In the instructive preface the editor remarks: "This collection of tunes has been made in the hope that it may render the collection of hymns entitled Gít Sangrah, to which it is adapted, more generally useful to the native congregations where those hymns are usually sung. The natives of Hindustan having no system of musical notation current among them, the native Christians are only able to learn the tunes of the hymns published for them by hearing them sung. In this volume melodies for the hymns in native metres in the Gít Sangrah are given in the usual musical notes; and if missionaries or others, who have the requisite skill, will acquire these tunes from the notes, and then sing them to the native congregations, they will find that they will learn them with much greater facility than English tunes, and sing them with particular pleasure. The air only of the tunes has been given, because it is not customary with the natives to sing more than one part. Almost all the melodies have been taken down as they are sung by the persons who either composed them or first sang them to Christian hymns, and no attempt has been made to improve or modify them. Those tunes which are distinguished by an asterisk are standard Hindu tunes taken down from professional singers."

A Telugu collection of tunes, called "Sangíta Ratnákaram," was printed at Madras by Vénugopál Nayakkar, in 1862.

The Chinese Airs which have been brought to Europe are not published in a separate collection. The same remark applies to the airs of the Siamese and Burmese. A number of Japanese airs, which P. F. von Siebold noted down during his sojourn in Japan, have been arranged for the pianoforte by J. Küffner (Leyden, 1836; oblong 8vo). Persian airs are contained in "Specimens of the Popular Poetry of Persia," by Alexander Chodzko (London: Allen and Co., 1842; 8vo). Airs of songs from Tunis and Algeria have been collected, and arranged for the pianoforte, by Salvador-Daniel (Paris: Richault; folio).

In America we have to notice the songs of the Canadian boatmen, who are hunters and fur traders, and are of French extraction. Several collections of these songs have been published in Canada and in the United States, such as "La Lyre Canadienne," "Chants de Voyageur Canadien," "Chansons Canadiens," &c. Many of the airs are old; some, which were brought to Canada by the French settlers about three hundred years ago, are still sung to the original French words. A selection of them which has appeared in England is entitled "Canadian Airs, collected by Lieutenant Back, R.N., during the late Arctic Expedition under Captain Franklin; with Symphonies and Accompaniments," by Edward Knight (London: J. Power, 1823; folio, two vols.). These airs have English poetry substituted for the original French poetry of the *voyageurs*.

In the United States we find among the popular songs several which evidently were imported into the western hemisphere by the German immigrants. The country is too young to possess old tunes of its own growth, if we except the airs of the Indian aborigines. No doubt, the ultimate characteristics of the national airs of the United States will depend much upon the songs which the children at the present time are taught to sing. A melody which we have learnt in early childhood, and with which pleasant recollections are associated, remains to us endeared through lifetime. The song-books for children, of which many have appeared in the United States, are therefore suggestive to the student of national music. As a curious specimen may be noticed "School Melodies; containing a choice Collection of Popular Airs, with original and appropriate words," by J. W. Greene (Boston, 1852; oblong 12mo). In the preface the editor says: "The leading characteristics of the present work are that the airs are almost exclusively popular;" and of one of the songs he remarks: "It has long been a favourite in the Boston schools." This little song, called "John Brown," is evidently intended to teach little children to count as far as ten. The tune to which it is sung is almost identical with the air of "O, dear! what can the matter be?" which was rather in vogue in London towards the end of the last century. However, the words are the most characteristic feature of the American ditty; for, the children, before they have learnt to count their ten fingers are led by it to regard an Indian child as if it were a puppy:—

> John Brown had a little Indian—
> Had a little Indian boy.
> One, two, three little Indian—
> Four, five, six little Indian—
> Seven, eight, nine little Indian—
> Ten little Indian boys.
> John Brown had ten little Indian—
> Ten little Indian boys.

The initiatory lesson embodied in this song perhaps explains certain conceptions which occur in a particular noteworthy book entitled "Slave Songs in the United States" (New York: Simpson and Co., 1867; royal 8vo), which affords an insight into Negro music. The greater number of the songs in this book were written down from the lips of the coloured people by its editors, W. F. Allen, C. P. Ware, and L. M. Garrison. A few of the songs were composed since the emancipation of the slaves; all the others are old. Most of them are sacred songs, the poetry being in the Negro dialect. Funny as this corrupted English may appear in certain humorous songs which one occasionally hears by so-called Negro minstrels in England, the impression it produces in the touching hymns and sacred songs is very different; there will probably be but few readers among those who peruse these artless and sincere effusions who will not be deeply impressed with the words as well as with the airs. In an annotation to the touching song called "Nobody knows de trouble I've had," we are told by the editors: "Once, when there had been a good deal of ill-feeling excited and trouble was apprehended, owing to the uncertain action of the Government in regard to the confiscated land on the Sea Islands, General Howard was called upon to address the coloured people earnestly and even severely. Sympathising with them, however, he could not speak to his own satisfaction; and to relieve their minds of the ever-present sense of injustice, and prepare them to listen, he asked them to sing. Immediately an old woman on the outskirts of the meeting began 'Nobody knows de trouble I've had,' and the whole audience joined. The General was so affected by the plaintive words and melody, that he found himself melting into tears, and quite unable to maintain his official sternness."

Turning to Mexico, we have especially to notice: "Coleccion de 24 Canciones y Jarabes Mexicanos, arreglados para Piano" (Hamburg: Böhme; folio), a publication which contains interesting specimens of those little Mexican airs in which an unaccented note of the bar is emphasised. To appreciate fully these charming melodies, one must imagine them sung, with the accompaniment of the guitar, by a sentimental serenader on a serene Mexican night. An attention to such associations is indispensable in order to ascertain exactly the true spirit of national songs. An inquirer who has no lively imagination, and is deficient in poetical conception, probably will not experience a high degree of enjoyment in the examination of these treasures.

In "Zwölf Brasilianische Volkslieder, herausgegeben von J. H. Clasing" (Hamburg: Cranz; oblong folio), we have a selection of Brazilian airs resembling the Portugese *modinha*, from which they are evidently an offspring. The "Alyra Pernambucana," by M. J. R. Vieira (Pernambuco; folio), consists of a series of popular pieces. Here may also be mentioned: "Seis Canciones Espanoles del Perú y Chile," edited by G. de la Perdiz (London, 1846; folio), which contains an English translation of the original words. Airs of the Indian aborigines in South America have been published in a Supplement to "Reise in Brasilien," by Spix and Martius (Munich, 1823; 4to), and in "Voyage dans l'Amérique Méridionale," by Alcide d'Orbigny (Paris, 1839-43). Twelve songs of the South American Indians, arranged for the pianoforte by C. E. Södling, have been published in Sweden (Stockholm: A. Hirsch; folio).

There remains a word to be said concerning the so-called transcriptions of national airs by eminent pianists. Some of these are very interesting. F. Liszt, for instance, has rendered the characteristics of the Hungarian music most faithfully; perhaps he succeeded in this all the better since he is himself a native of Hungary. However, the present division of our research is already so long, that I am loth to enter upon any topic which is of secondary importance for the object in view.

POETRY.

NATIONAL poetry is so closely associated with national music that it must not be entirely ignored here. In the books of poetry the musician will often find the words to those airs of songs which have been printed separately; and without an acquaintance with the words it is generally impossible to form a correct opinion of the air. Besides, many of the books of poetry contain introductory essays or annotations, in which an account is given of the music and manner of singing of the people whose poetry is discussed.

Carefully edited publications of this kind are of earlier date, and are more numerous, than carefully edited publications of national tunes. Musicians have been in this respect rather behind the poets and scientific men. In Germany it was especially J. G. von Herder, during the latter half of the eighteenth century, who gave an impulse to a more universal research by his German translation of songs of different nations (Leipzig, 1778), of which a new edition by Johannes Falk appeared in the year 1825, and again another in 1840. Among subsequent German compilers of similar works deserves to be particularly named O. L. B. Wolff, whose "Halle der Völker" (Frankfurt a/M., 1837) and "Hausschatz der Volkspoesie" (Leipzig, 1853; fourth edition) contain metrical translations of national songs from many countries. Moreover, to the musician perhaps the most useful publication of this kind written in German is a dissertation entitled "Versuch einer geschichtlichen Charakteristik der Volkslieder germanischer Nationen," by Talvj (Leipzig, 1840; 8vo), which contains specimens of songs of uncivilised races as well as of European nations. Talvj is the wife of the well-known American scholar, Edward Robinson; her maiden name was Therese Amalie Louise von Jacob, from the initials of which she formed the *nom de plume* Talvj. It would require much space, and would probably interest but few musicians, were I to insert here the titles of even only the most important collections of national poetry which have been printed in different countries. I shall, however, give the names of some of the principal editors, and the date of publication of their works; thus the student will be enabled easily to find any book he desires to consult on the subject under consideration:—

Denmark.—Adam Oehlenschläger (Copenhagen, 1841). Svend Grundtvig (Copenhagen, 1853).

Faroe Isles.—H. C. Lyngbye (Randers, 1822).

Germany.—Arnim and Brentano, "Des Knaben Wunderhorn" (Heidelberg, 1806; second edition, 1846; third edition, Berlin, 1857). J. G. Meinert (Vienna and Hamburg, 1817). F. K. von Erlach (Mannheim, 1834). L. von Soltau (Leipzig, 1836). J. Görres (Frankfurt a/M., 1817). L. Uhland (Stuttgart and Tübingen, 1844). P. M. Körner (Stuttgart, 1840).

The Netherlands.—Le Jeune (The Hague, 1828). J. A. A. Thijm (Amsterdam, 1850).

France.—Lerous de Lincy (Paris, 1841). Silvestre (Paris, 1840). P. Paris (Paris, 1833). "La Fleur des Chansons Nouvelles" (Lyons, 1586; new edition, Paris, 1830). C. Nisard (Paris, 1867).

Italy.—N. Tommaseo (Venice, 1841). A. Alverà (Venice, 1844). C. Nigra (Turin, 1858). E. S. Righi (Verona, 1863). Marcoaldi (Genoa, 1855). G. Tigri (Florence, 1860). L. Vigo (Catania, 1857). Visconti (Rome, 1830). Dalmedico (Venice, 1857). G. Pitrè (Palermo, 1870). E. Rubieri (Florence, 1877).

Spain.—D. Preciso (Madrid, 1799). A. Duran (Madrid, 1832). Don T. Segarra (Leipzig, 1862). F. del Castillo (Valencia, 1511). F. del Castillo (Amberes, 1555). D. L. de Fortajada (Valencia, about 1600). L. de Sepulveda (Amberes, 1566). A. de Villalta (Valencia, 1595). M. de Madrigal (Valladolid, 1605). Böhl de Faber (Hamburg, 1821). J. Grimm (Vienna, 1831).

Portugal.—Almeida-Garrett (Lisbon, 1851).

Peru.—José Toribio Polo (Lima, 1862).

Greece.—C. Fauriel (Paris, 1824). Lemercier (Paris,

1824). Marcellus (Paris, 1860). The three works here alluded to contain French metrical translations of popular songs of the modern Greeks.

Servia.—S. K. Vuk (Leipzig, 1823; and Vienna, 1833). Simeon Milutinowitch (Leipzig, 1826).

Montenegro and Herzegovina.—T. Tshoikowitch (Leipzig, 1837). J. Milownk (Ofen, 1833).

Dalmatia.—O. A. Kacic-Miosic (Zara, 1861).

Illyria.—A. Mickievicz (Zara, 1860).

Roumania.—B. Alexandri (Jassy, 1853). A. Marienesen (Pesth, 1858).

Bulgaria and Roumelia.—A collection of the poetical traditions of the Bulgarians and Thracians has been published by Professor Geitler of Agram, in the year 1878. This work is based upon Verdovich's " Veda Slovenâ " and the same scholar's hitherto unprinted collections, and also on the compiler's own investigations.

Hungary.—J. Kollar (Buda, 1834). J. Erdély (Pesth, 1846).

Transylvania.—J. K. Schuller (Hermannstadt, 1840). F. W. Schuster (Hermannstadt, 1865).

The national songs of Little-Russia (including the Ukraine, Volyhnia, and Podolia) are in a peculiar Russian dialect. Collections of them have been published by the following editors: Tzertelef, 1819; Maximovitch, three books, 1827, 1837, 1843; Sreznefski, 1833, and 1838; Metlinski, 1857; Kostomarof, 1859; Zakrefski, 1860.

The Chumaks are wandering carriers who, with their carts drawn by oxen, travel to the Crimea to fetch salt, and to the Black Sea and the Sea of Azof to fetch fish for sale in the villages of the Ukraine. These carriers have peculiar songs of their own, a collection of which has recently been published, in Kief, edited by J. Y. Rudchenko, and entitled " Chumatskiya Narodnuiya Pyesni."

Several of the collections in languages little cultivated in England, or selections from them, have been translated into German; and, as these may be found preferable, the most important of them shall be indicated here:—

" Altdänische Heldenlieder, Balladen und Märchen übersetzt von W. C. Grimm " (Heidelberg, 1811; 8vo).

"Volkslieder der Schweden, von G. Mohnike" (Berlin, 1830; 8vo). "Altschwedische Balladen, von G. Mohnike" (Stuttgart, 1836; 8vo). "Schwedische Volksharfe, von J. L. Studach" (Stockholm, 1826; sm. 8vo). This interesting book contains also some airs in notation.

"Schwedische Volkslieder der Vorzeit, von Rosa Warrens" (Leipzig, 1857; 12mo). Contains some airs. "Norwegische Islandische, Färöische Volkslieder, &c., von Rosa Warrens" (Hamburg, 1866; sm. 8vo).

"Alt-islandische Volks-Balladen und Heldenlieder der Färinger, von P. P. Willatzen" (Bremen, 1865; sm. 8vo). Most of the old Icelandic ballads in this work are translated from "Islenzk Fornkvädi ved Svend Grundtvig og Jón Sigurdsson" (Copenhagen, 1854).

"Niederländische Volkslieder, von Hoffman von Fallersleben" (Hanover, 1856; 8vo).

A collection of *Oudvlaemsche Liederen*, comprising 145 songs of the fourteenth and fifteenth centuries, was published in the year 1848 by a society of Flemish antiquarians.

"Altfranzösische Volkslieder, mit Anmerkungen von O. L. B. Wolff" (Leipzig, 1831; 12mo).

"Volkslieder und Romanzen der Spanier, von Emanuel Geibel" (Berlin, 1840; sm. 8vo).

"Portugiesische Volkslieder von C. F. Bellermann" (Leipzig, 1854; 12mo). "Die alten Liederbücher der Portugiesen, von C. F. Bellermann" (Berlin, 1840; 4to).

"Proben Portugiesischer und Catalanischer Volksromanzen, von F. Wolf" (Vienna, 1856; 8vo).

"Anthologie neugriechischer Volkslieder, von Theodor Kind" (Leipzig, 1861; 12mo).

"Neugriechische Volksgesänge, von J. M. Firmenich" (Berlin, 1840; 8vo).

"Liebes-und Klagelieder des neugriechischen Volkes, von A. Passow" (Magdeburg, 1861; 8vo).

"Stimmen des russischen Volks, von P. von Goetze" (Stuttgart, 1828; 8vo).

"Die Balalaika; Russische Volkslieder, von Julius Altmann" (Berlin, 1863; 12mo).

"Die poetische Ukraine, eine Sammlung Kleinrussischer Volkslieder, von F. Bodenstedt" (Stuttgart, 1845; 8vo).

"Ehstnische Volkslieder, von H. Neus" (Reval, 1850; 8vo). Esthonian popular songs, in the original and with a German translation, published by the Esthonian Literary Society.

"Runen finnischer Volkspoesie, von Julius Altmann" (Leipzig, 1856; sm. 8vo).

"Volkslieder der Serben, von Talvj" (Leipzig, 1853; sm. 8vo, two vols.).

"Die Gesänge der Serben, von S. Kapper" (Leipzig, 1852; sm. 8vo, two vols.).

"Serbische Hochzeitslieder, von E. E. Wesely" (Pesth, 1826; 8vo).

"Gusle; Serbische Nationallieder, von L. A. Frankl" (Vienna, 1852; 8vo).

"Romänische Volkslieder, von J. K. Schuller" (Hermannstadt, 1859; 12mo).

"Ungarische Volkslieder, von M. A. Greguss" (Leipzig, 1846; sm. 8vo).

"Slawische Volkslieder, von J. Wenzig" (Halle, 1830; 12mo).

"Altcechische Leiche, Lieder und Sprüche, von Julius Feifalik" (Vienna, 1862; 8vo).

"Sammlung altböhmischer lyrisch-epischer Gesänge, von W. A. Swaboda" (Prague, 1829; 8vo).

"Böhmische Granaten, von Alfred Waldau" (Prague, 1858; 12mo, two vols.).

"Agrumi; volksthümliche Poesien aus allen Mundarten Italiens, von A. Kopisch" (Berlin, 1838; sm. 8vo).

"Volkslieder aus Venetien, von A. Wolf" (Vienna, 1864; 8vo).

"Italienisches Liederbuch, von Paul Heyse" (Berlin, 1860; 8vo).

"Proben der Volkslitteratur der Türkischen Stämme Süd-Sibiriens, von W. Radloff" (St. Petersburg, 1866; 8vo).

"Die Wüstenharfe; eine Sammlung arabischer Volkslieder, von J. Altmann" (Leipzig, 1856; 8vo).

"Hamâsa; oder die ältesten arabischen Volkslieder, von F. Rückert" (Stuttgart, 1846; 8vo, two vols.).

"Schi-King, Chinesisches Liederbuch, von F. Rückert" (Altona, 1833; 8vo).
"Schi-King, für's Deutsche Volk, herausgegeben, von J. Cramer" (Crefeld, 1844; 8vo).

This may be the place to notice an interesting publication entitled "Germaniens Völkerstimmen; Sammlung der deutschen Mundarten in Dichtungen, Sagen, Mährchen, Volksliedern, &c.," edited by J. M. Firmenich (Berlin, 1843-66; three vols. royal 8vo; with an Appendix, Berlin, 1867). This important work, compiled under the auspices of the King of Prussia, contains popular songs in various dialects of the German language, but without the airs. Many contributions of popular poetry were sent to the editor, in answer to his appeal in public papers, from different districts of Germany, and even from German colonists in foreign countries, who, living together in villages, as they did in their fatherland, have retained their mother-tongue. In the year 1851, Napoleon, then President of the French Republic, resolved to have a similar work for France entitled "Recueil Général des Poésies Populaires de la France." A decree referring to it, which appeared in the *Moniteur* of September 16, 1852, has, among other introductory remarks by H. Fortoul, the Minister of Public Instruction, the following; "Les chants populaires ont été, depuis le commencement du siècle, l'objet des recherches de l'érudition. Notre pays possède, plus qu'aucun autre, de précieux restes de ces poésies, aussi bien dans la langue nationale que dans les idiomes provinciaux qu'elle a remplacés. Malheureusement ces richesses, que le temps emporte chaque jour, disparaîtront bientôt, si l'on ne s'empresse de recueillir tant de témoignages touchants de la gloire et des malheurs de notre patrie."

These projects are also important to musicians, although they interest to a higher degree philologists and ethnologists. It would be an advantage to art as well as to science if the English Government would follow in this respect the example of the Germans and the French. Considering the great number of different races included in the British empire the result might be highly instructive. The Russian Government has perhaps done most to encourage such investigations; and as there are many different races subject to Russia in Europe and Asia, a rich harvest has been obtained. England has hitherto done the least in this field of inquiry as regards science and still less as regards art.

Perhaps not many English musicians will care for the foreign publications of national poetry; however, books of this kind published in English may prove more interesting or, at any rate, more intelligible. The following are only a few out of a considerable number :—

Alexander Prior: "Ancient Danish Ballads translated from the Originals" (London, 1860; 8vo, two vols.). The translations have been made from Svend Grundtvig's "Danmarks Gamle Folkeviser," and from "Udvalgte Danske Viser fra Middelalderen," edited by Abrahamson, Nyerup, and Rahbek. The latter work has already been mentioned in the present essay. S. Grundtvig's edition of the Danish popular songs, published under commission of the Danish Government, gives, besides many hitherto unknown ballads, more correct readings of the old ones already known, and contains much research and valuable information respecting Scandinavian national poetry in general.

Grenville Murray: "Doine; or the National Songs and Legends of Roumania" (London, 1854; sm. 8vo).

Owen Meredith: "Serbski Pesme: or National Songs of Servia" (London, 1861; sm. 8vo).

W. R. S. Ralston: "The Songs of the Russian People, as illustrative of Slavonic Mythology and Russian Social Life" (London, 1872; 8vo).

Sir John Bowring: "Servian Popular Poetry" (London, 1827; 8vo); "Specimens of the Polish Poets" (London, 1827; 8vo); "Specimens of the Russian Poets" (London, 1821; 8vo, two vols.); "Poetry of the Magyars" (London, 1830; 8vo); "Cheskian Anthology, History of the Poetry of Bohemia" (London, 1832; 8vo); "Ancient Poetry and Romances of Spain" (London, 1824; 8vo).

Thomas Rodd: "Ancient Spanish Ballads" (London, 1812; 8vo, two vols.).

J. G. Lockhart: "Ancient Spanish Ballads, Historical

and Romantic" (London, 1823; sm. 4to: illustrated edition, London, 1841; 4to).

C. B. Sheridan: "Songs of the Greeks, from the Romaic Text, edited by C. Fauriel, with additions, translated into English verse" (London, 1825; 8vo). The title of Fauriel's work is "Chants populaires de la Grèce moderne" (Paris, 1824; 8vo, two vols.). There is also a German translation of Fauriel's work, by Wilhelm Müller, entitled "Neugriechische Volkslieder, übersetzt und mit des französischen Herausgebers eigenen Erläuterungen versehen" (Leipzig, 1825; 8vo, two vols.).

Leo M. Alishan: "Armenian Popular Songs translated into English" (Venice, St. Lazarus, 1852; 8vo).

Ebenezer Pocock: "Flowers of the East; with an Introductory Sketch of Oriental Poetry and Music" (London, 1833; sm. 8vo). Contains Persian poems translated into English.

F. V. Dickens: "Hyak Nin Ts'shiu, or Stanzas by a Century of Poets; being Japanese Lyrical Songs, translated into English, with explanatory notes" (London: Smith, Elder and Co., 1866; 8vo).

However faithfully the translation of a poem conceived in a foreign language may have been rendered, it is of course impossible to reproduce unimpaired all the characteristics of the original. A lover of music who has no opportunity of becoming acquainted with a symphony by Beethoven as it was originally composed for the orchestra, will be glad to have recourse to a pianoforte arrangement, imperfectly though it reveals the conceptions of the composer. A translation of a foreign poem might perhaps not improperly be likened to an arrangement of a musical composition. The following works contain poetry in its original language:—

Robert Jamieson: "Popular Ballads and Songs" (Edinburgh, 1806; 8vo, two vols.).

William Motherwell: "Minstrelsy Ancient and Modern, with an Historical Introduction and Notes" (Glasgow, 1826; 4to). The work contains also some Scotch tunes.

W. E. Aytoun: "Ballads of Scotland" (Edinburgh, 1858; 12mo, two vols.).

P. Buchan: "Ancient Ballads and Songs of the North of Scotland" (Edinburgh, 1828; 8vo, two vols.).

J. Pinkerton: "Select Scottish Ballads" (London, 1783; sm. 8vo, two vols.).

J. Gilchrist: "A Collection of Ancient and Modern Scottish Ballads, Tales, and Songs" (Edinburgh, 1815; 12mo, two vols.).

Sir Walter Scott: "Minstrelsy of the Scottish Border" (Edinburgh, 1810; 8vo, three vols.; fourth edition).

James Hardiman: "Irish Minstrelsy, or Bardic Remains of Ireland" (London, 1831; 8vo, two vols.).

T. Crofton Croker: "The Popular Songs of Ireland" (London, 1839; 8vo).

Charlotte Brooke: "Reliques of Irish Poetry, translated into English Verse, with Notes and the Originals in the Irish character" (Dublin, 1789; 4to).

Duncathail: "Street Ballads, Popular Poetry, and Household Songs of Ireland" (Dublin, 1865; 12mo; second edition).

Thomas Evans: "Old Ballads, Historical and Narrative" (London, 1777; 8vo, four vols.); a new edition by R. H. Evans (London, 1810; 8vo, four vols.).

Robert Bell: "Early Ballads" (London, 1856; 12mo).

John Bell: "Rhymes of Northern Bards; being a Collection of Old and New Songs and Poems peculiar to the Counties of Newcastle-upon-Tyne, Northumberland, and Durham" (Newcastle-upon-Tyne, 1812). Similar publications by G. Henderson and J. Harland have been already mentioned in this essay.

J. H. Dixon: "Ancient Poems, Ballads, and Songs of the Peasantry of England" (London, 1846; 8vo).

J. Payne Collier: "Book of Roxburghe Ballads" (London, 1847; sm. 4to).

The collections of ancient popular poetry by Thomas Percy, Joseph Ritson, &c.

J. O. Halliwell: "The Nursery Rhymes of England" (London, 1853; 8vo; sixth edition). Nursery rhymes, with the tunes to which they are still sung in the nurseries of England, have been published by E. F. Rimbault and others.

G. P. Morris: "American Melodies; containing a Single

Selection from the Productions of Two Hundred Writers" (Philadelphia, 1840; 12mo). The title of this book is rather misleading: the musical inquirer must not expect to find any tunes in notation; the book contains only the poetry of the most popular songs in the United States at the beginning of the present century.

Frank Moore: " Rebel Rhymes and Rhapsodies, collected and edited " (New York, 1864; 12mo).

A remark of a foreigner touching upon the vagueness with which English musicians use certain terms relating to their art ought perhaps not to be offered without an apology, since a foreigner is not likely to understand the English language so well as an English musician. But a modest suggestion may perhaps be pardonable. Howbeit, it seems strange that English musicians do not make a distinction between the designation of *song* and *ballad*, but use the terms indiscriminately. At all events, many so-called ballads in English music-books are not ballads artistically speaking, but are lyric songs of the kind which the Germans call *Lied*. A ballad is an epic poem with or without music; and thus is the term used by Jamieson, Ritson, and other scientific men, in their publications of popular poetry in the English language. It is not so unimportant as it may appear at a first glance that musicians also should clearly discern between the terms which they employ in their art.

DANCE-TUNES.

The instrumental tunes of national dances are frequently derived from the airs of songs. In fact, among uncivilised nations the music to which dances are performed consists very often of songs, the rhythmical effect of which is enhanced by the loud steps of the dancers, by clapping of hands, or by the employment of some instrument of percussion, as castanets, drums, &c. The tunes of national dances which have been published in European countries are mostly arranged for the pianoforte. However, as many of the collections of national songs before mentioned contain also dance-tunes, it is hardly necessary here to give a long list of the separate collections which have appeared in print. Most of them have been compiled with too little regard to the preservation of the original characteristics of the music to be of essential use for study.

Some insight into the variety of national dances may be obtained by an examination of a publication entitled " Volkstänze aller Nationen der Erde," edited by Louis Köhler (Brunswick : Meyer and Litolff ; folio), which contains 120 dance-tunes arranged for the pianoforte. The publication has rather an assumptious title, professing to comprise popular dance-tunes of all nations. This is not the place to enumerate all the dances in the world known to be in popular use ; most readers, did they see a list of the names of the dances, would probably be surprised at the great number of them, each designating a particular dance having its own music. Alfred Waldau, in his little book entitled " Böhmische Nationaltänze ; Culturstudie " (Prague : H. Dominikus, 1859 ; 12mo), describes about fifty different dances of the villagers in Bohemia. It would appear that the Bohemians are extraordinarily fond of dancing ; at any rate, an equal number of dances has hitherto not been collected in France, Spain, Mexico, or in some other countries where the people are notoriously much addicted to dancing.

No doubt several of the specimens enumerated by A. Waldau among the popular ones of Bohemia were imported into that country, and therefore cannot be strictly regarded as national dances of the Bohemians. Indeed, it is often more difficult to trace the original home of a dance-tune than of the air of a national song; the former, being instrumental and unfettered by words, is more easily transferred from one country to another and more readily adopted by different nations.

In England, about three centuries ago, we find several dances in popular use which were derived from the Continent. It hardly admits of a doubt that their continental tunes were imported with them; though afterwards other tunes more or less similar to the original ones were substituted by English musicians. The old collection of dance-tunes, the first edition of which was published in London about the middle of the seventeenth century, under the title of " The English Dancing Master," contains specimens of such dances of foreign origin. The work, having gone through many editions, with enlargements, comprised, about the year 1720, three volumes oblong 8vo, and its title was altered into "The Compleat Country Dancing Master." Several other curious collections appeared in London during the eighteenth century; of these, by way of example, may be noticed:—

"The Newest Minuets, Rigadoons, and French Dances for the year 1721, perform'd at Court and Publick Entertainm^{ts}; composed by Mr. Murphy. To which is added the Ball Dances perform'd at Schools; the tunes proper for the Violin, Hoboy, or Flute" (London; oblong 8vo). The work contains, besides tunes of Murphy's composition, several popular ones.

"Minuets with the Basses for His Majesty's Birth Day, as they were perform'd at the Ball at Court; the tunes proper for the Violin, German Flute, or Harpsichord" (London: T. Walsh, 1738; oblong 8vo).

"Twenty-four Country-Dances for the year 1787; with proper tunes and directions to each dance, as they are performed at Court, Bath, and all Public Amusements" (London: J. Preston; oblong 8vo).

"A Collection of New Minuets for the year 1788; perform'd

at Court, Bath, and all Publick Assemblys; set for the Harpsichord, Violin, German Flute or Hautboy. London: printed for Samuel, Ann, and Peter Thompson, No. 75, St. Paul's Church Yard; where may be had: Thompson's Compleat Collection of 800 favourite Country Dances, in 4 vols.; Thompson's Compleat Collection of 400 favourite Minuets for the Harpsichord, in 4 vols.; Thompson's Dances and Cotillons for the Harpsichord; Sandro's Cotillons dedicated to the Prince Royal; De Latre's Cotillons."

Suggestive examples of an early importation of foreign dances into Holland are to be found in a publication of Dutch dance-tunes, entitled: "Het derde musyck boexken begrepen ghetal van onser neder duytscher spraken, daer inne begrepen syn alder hande danserye, te vuetens Basse-dansen, Ronden, Allemaingien, Pauanen, end meer andere, mits oeck vyfthien nieuvue gaillarden, zeer lustich ende bequaem om spelen op alle musicale Instrumētē," by Tielman Susato (Antwerp, 1551; sm. 4to). As this publication is a hundred years older than the "English Dancing Master," it would even for this reason deserve particular attention, were it not on account of some curiosities which it contains. One of the tunes, headed *La Morisque*, is probably the oldest tune of the famous Morris-dance still extant. As it is interesting from having been printed in the year 1550, when most likely it was already an old tune, it shall be inserted here—not in its old notation of square-shaped notes with the C clef on the second line, and without any division of bars, but in our present usual notation, which is at a glance intelligible to modern musicians:—

Surely, this tune does not appear very much as if it were above three hundred years old. If a pianoforte accompaniment were made to it in the Thalbergian manner, it might pass for a modern drawing-room piece; and the same remark applies to several others of the tunes in this old Dutch book. *La Morisque*, to judge from its name, was probably introduced into the Netherlands from France. It is a well-known fact that the Morris-dance, supposed to have been originally derived from the Moors in Spain, became during the latter period of the Middle Ages diffused through many European countries. It is still occasionally performed in England; likewise in Alsace, where it is called *Morisken;* and especially in the island of Corsica, where it is called *Moresca*, and is danced by men in armour who represent a conflict between the Moors and the Christians. As regards the *Basse-danssen*, of which there are several tunes in the old Dutch book in question, it may suffice to know that this is the kind of dance in which the performers moved slowly about, scarcely raising their feet from the ground. It was rather an aristocratic dance, being especially in favour with the higher classes of society.

In Germany also there are some published collections of popular dance-tunes which date as far back as the sixteenth century. The circumstances of such tunes being printed in some of the instruction-books for playing the organ has given rise in modern time to the supposition that dance-tunes were played in the Church. This appears, however, to be an erroneous notion, which may be dispelled by an examination of the old books. It was not unusual for gentlemen of some means to have a little organ in their house for playing secular music as well as for accompanying devotional songs. In the beginning of the sixteenth century the organ-builder Georg Voll, in Nürnberg, constructed small organs for domestic use and portable organs of the kind which were called *Regals*. He even made them in a case having the shape of a book: such a little instrument, in outward appearance not unlike a large German bible, was called *Bibelregal*. If the reader visited the Exhibition of Ancient Musical Instruments which was held in the South Kensington

Museum in the year 1872, he will perhaps remember the *Bibelregal*, about three hundred years old, which was lent to the Exhibition by an English gentleman, in whose possession it is. A German book on organ-playing, entitled "Orgel oder Instrument Tabulatur," by E. N. Ammerbach (Leipzig, 1571; sm. 4to), contains, besides sacred pieces, a number of popular dance-tunes. This work I have not seen; but C. F. Becker, in his "Hausmusik in Deutschland" ("Music in the House in Germany," Leipzig, 1840; 4to), describes it circumstantially, and notices especially a fine wood-engraving, facing the title-page, which represents the master of the house and his wife with their guests seated at a long table at the far end of the room; servants, headed by a major-domo, are bringing in wine and various dishes; to the left in the foreground is the orchestra, consisting of players on flutes, cornets, and trombones, who are accompanying a chorus of singers; and to the right is an organ, played by a gentleman who carries a long sword at his side, and whose head is ornamented with a handsome baret. The organ has three registers: and a boy standing behind the table is engaged in blowing the little bellows.

Another German book of that period containing dance-tunes is by Bernhard Schmid, an organist of Strassburg, and bears the title "*Zwey Bücher einer Neuen Kunstlichen Tabulatur, auff Orgel vnd Instrument*," &c. (Strassburg, 1577; folio). The dances of which the tunes are given in this publication are most of them German, and others are of foreign origin. Like those given by Ammerbach, the German dances are in $\frac{4}{4}$ time, each of them having appended to it a so-called *Proportio*, which is in $\frac{3}{4}$ time. In Bernhard Schmid's book the designation *Proportio* is corrupted into *Proportz*, and is also called *Hopeldantz*, *Hupfauff*, &c.—names which indicate that it was performed with a hopping step; and it appears probable that the present German dance called *Hopser* derived its name from the same circumstance. Moreover Bernhard Schmid calls the *Proportio* also *Saltarello* and *Nachdantz;* the former name is Italian, and the latter, which is German, signifies an appended dance.

No doubt, the introduction of extraneous matter into a discussion is generally objectionable as it is an impediment to the contemplated aim. There are, however, exceptional instances, in which a few steps aside from the road may not be amiss, were it only to pluck a wild flower. Although I cannot assume to offer the reader anything so pleasant as this, I believe, considering how little is known of the life of the famous " Father Smith," English organists and musical antiquarians will readily pardon a short divergence called forth by the name of the editor of the old dance-tunes just noticed. The celebrated English organ-builder Smith was a native of Germany. His German name was Bernhard Schmid (or Schmidt). He came to England about the year 1660, accompanied by his nephews Gerhard and Bernhard Christian, who worked with him. He was called Father Smith to distinguish him from his nephews ; and perhaps also, as Dr. Burney states in his " History of Music," " to express the reverence due to his abilities, which placed him at the head of his profession." As he was so highly appreciated, it is rather singular that hardly any biographical notice of the man has been transmitted to us. The name Schmidt is as common in Germany as Smith is in England ; and this perhaps accounts for the birthplace of Father Smith being unknown. His Christian name is, however, not so common. There were two organists of the name of Bernhard Schmidt in the Thomas Church at Strassburg, during the second half of the sixteenth century. The profession of organ-builder was not unfrequently combined with that of organ-player. For instance, Johann Daniel Silbermann, in 1746, and Johann Heinrich Silbermann, in 1754, two sons of the well-known Andreas Silbermann—and likewise Johann Friedrich Silbermann, a grandson of Andreas—practised both professions. Thus also Father Smith, who was organist at St. Margaret's, Westminster. Insufficient as this circumstantial evidence is to determine the original home of Father Smith, it may put the inquirer upon the right track. Andreas Silbermann, born in Saxony, in the year 1678, was the elder brother of the famous Gottfried Silbermann, and the father of a large family of organ-builders. Having settled in Strassburg, he married, in the year 1708, Anne Maria Schmidt—perhaps a relation of Father Smith. These hints must suffice. It is impossible to expatiate here upon a subject which, considering the name involved in it, would lead to endless inquiries.

Neither will it be necessary to enlarge upon the artistic employment of national dance-tunes by our classical composers, as shown in the old Suites and such-like publications. These may be supposed to be well-known to every musician who has studied his art. It may, however, interest the reader to have his attention drawn to the continual change in fashion to which even national dances are subjected. Scarcely any of the dances which were so much admired by our forefathers a century or two ago are still in popular favour; and although in some districts of European countries genuine national dances of high antiquity have not entirely yielded to the influence of modern civilisation, there is reason to surmise that they will gradually experience the same decay which has already been, to a great extent, the fate of the old and characteristic usages, notions, poetry, and music of the people. In fact, many of the national dances of the present time are comparatively of modern origin. For instance the *Bolero*, which, from its wide-spread popularity in some countries of America as well as in Spain, might be supposed to be a very old Spanish dance, is, according to some musical historians, an invention of Don Sebastian Zerezo, dating from about the year 1780. However this may be, it is not exactly a new invention, but rather a modification of the *Seguidilla*, an old Spanish dance which is performed to a song.

The *Polka*, which in the present century has had its run through almost every civilised country, is only about fifty years old. According to A. Waldau, who relates its history in his little book already mentioned, it was invented about the year 1830, by a country lass in Bohemia, who was in service with a citizen in Elbe-Teinitz. Josef Neruda, the schoolmaster of that little town, happening to witness the performance of the dance by the girl, which she had contrived merely for her own amusement, wrote down the tune as she sang it while dancing. The new dance soon found admirers in Elbe-Teinitz, and in the year 1835 it made its way into Prague, the Bohemian metropolis, where it received the name *Polka*, probably on account of the half-step occurring in the dance; for the Bohemian word *Pulka* designates " the half." Four years later, its tune, which had now become a great favourite in Prague, was carried to Vienna by a military band which, under the direction of the able bandmaster Pregler, in Prague had obtained some reputation, and which visited Vienna in the year 1839. The Polka became now rapidly known throughout Austria. In 1840 it was danced the first time at the Odéon, a theatre in Paris, by Raab, a dancing-master from Prague. Here it found so much favour that it was introduced with astonishing rapidity into the most elegant and fashionable dancing saloons and private balls of Paris. From France it spread over all Europe, and even through North America. Celebrated composers wrote new tunes to it, and the original tune, which the girl sang, now seems to be lost.

The reader may judge from these statements how difficult it must be in many instances to ascertain the original home of a popular dance-tune. In truth, most of the published collections of national dance-tunes contain some specimens which do not properly belong to the country to which they are assigned. It is seldom that these publications include annotations, or even indications which might assist the student. There are, however, a few praiseworthy exceptions. Take, for instance, " A Collection of the Dance Music of Ireland, consisting of upwards of One Hundred National Jigs, Reels, Hornpipes, &c, arranged with easy basses for the pianoforte," by R. M. Levey (London : Jefferys, 1858 ; folio). This book, too, contains some melodies which are known not to be genuine Irish ; but the editor shows, from certain remarks in his Preface, that he is familiar with the peculiar features of the Irish music, and that his special endeavour has been to preserve the tunes intact.

Furthermore, in order to appreciate correctly a national dance-tune, an acquaintance with the usual manner of its performance is even more indispensable than it is in catching the true spirit of a national song. Let us take, for example, a Spanish Fandango arranged for the pianoforte, as it is usually presented to the musical world. To obtain from such an arrangement a right impression of the effect of the music in its original condition, we must know that it is played on the guitar to the flexible and graceful movements and pantomimic action of a male and a female dancer, holding in their hands castanets, which they clatter at certain stages of the dance. We must be able to imagine the picturesque costume of the dancers and of the spectators, who on a Spanish summer evening are assembled on a lawn illuminated by torches, the air being scented by fragrant flowers.

Some of the numerous treatises on the art of dancing which have been published contain descriptions of dances appertaining to uncivilised races. In "A Treatise of the Art of Dancing;" by Giovanni Andrea Gallini (London, 1772; 8vo), the student will find a whole chapter on the subject. Much more accurate information, respecting the social habits and amusements of savages in different parts of the world has been obtained since that treatise was published. A small handy book, written in German, and recently issued, may be recommended as useful to inquirers in this branch of national music, although it treats chiefly on the obsolete dances of our ancestors. The title of the book is "Geschichte der Tanzkunst bei den cultivirten Völkern" by Albert Czerwinski (Leipzig: Weber, 1862; 8vo). There is also a chapter on national dances in my book entitled "An Introduction to the Study of National Music, comprising researches into popular songs, traditions, and customs" (London: Longmans and Co., 1866; 8vo). In this book the student will find the titles of many works which, for the sake of brevity, are in the present survey only indicated by the name of the author and the place and date of publication.

There are, besides dance-tunes, some other instrumental pieces which deserve to be classed with national music in a strict sense of the term. Several uncivilised nations have instrumental performances in processions, in warlike exploits, in religious ceremonies, and so on. For some account of such performances the student has to peruse the usual narrations of travellers and of residents in foreign countries, of which presently some remarks will be submitted for his consideration.

SACRED MUSIC.

It would be a mistake to assume that national music partakes exclusively of a secular character. This is far from being the case. Almost every European nation possesses sacred songs not used in divine worship which are genuine national songs. Some of the collections before mentioned contain specimens of such compositions; and, in Germany, several collections of popular sacred songs have been published separately, as is the case, for instance, in the following books :—

"Geistliche Volkslieder mit ihren ursprünglichen Weisen" (Paderborn : F. Schöningk, 1850 ; 4to). This collection was compiled by Freiherr von Haxthausen, partly from verbal communication and partly from old hymn-books. It may however be doubted whether all the airs are, as the title professes, those which originally belonged to the words.

"Cantica Spiritualia ; oder Auswahl der schönsten geistlichen Lieder," &c. (Augsburg, 1845, and Munich, 1847 ; 4to, two vols.). The songs are mostly taken from Roman Catholic hymn-books of previous centuries. The airs are printed with a pianoforte accompaniment. Probably but few of them, if any, are still in the mouths of the people ; but the publication may assist in rendering them popular again.

"Geistliche Volkslieder aus alter und neuerer Zeit, mit ihren Singweisen," by Friedrich Hommel (Leipzig : B. G. Teubner, 1864 ; 8vo). The editor states in his preface that in this collection all centuries, from the thirteenth to the present, are represented, and that it includes songs which are still in common use with the people of Bavaria. The airs are given in two-part harmony without any instrumental accompaniment, as the people are in the habit of singing them.

In Germany the *Weihnachtslieder*, or Christmas Carols, form probably the majority of the songs of this description ;

and the same appears to be the case in other European countries. English Christmas Carols with the tunes have been edited, in London, by E. F. Rimbault, J. Stainer, and others. Particularly noteworthy for reference are :—
"Christmas Carols, ancient and modern; including the most popular in the West of England, and the airs to which they are sung. Also specimens of French Provincial Carols; with an introduction and notes," by William Sandys (London, 1833; 8vo). And, by the same author: "Christmastide; its History, Festivities, and Carols" (London, no date; 8vo). This book contains, in an appendix, a number of airs arranged in three-part harmony.

"Songs and Carols; printed from a Manuscript of the Fifteenth Century," by Thomas Wright (London, 1842; 8vo).

As regards the *Noëls*, or Christmas Carols of France, several carefully compiled collections have been printed; take for instance: "Les Noëls Bressans de Bourg, de Pont-de-Vaux et des paroisses voisines, &c., par Philibert Le Duc" (Bourg-en-Bresse, 1845; sm. 8vo). "Airs des Noëls Lorrains, &c., par R. Grosjean" (Saint-Dié-des-Vosges, 1862; 4to). "Recueil des Noëls anciens au patois de Besançon" (Besançon, 1852; 8vo). "Noëls nouveaux sur des vieux airs, par C. Ribault de Laugardière" (Bourges, 1857; 8vo). "Recueil des Noëls composés en Langue Provençal par Nicolas Saboly, avec les airs notés, &c., par F. Seguin" (Avignon, 1856; folio).

A published collection of Welsh Christmas Carols bears the title "Caniadau Bethlehem," and is edited by J. D. Jones (Ruthin, 1857; 12mo). Specimens of Slavonic Christmas Carols are given in "Pastoralki i Koledy," &c., by the Abbé Michel-Martin Mioduszewski (Cracow, 1843; 8vo). This interesting book contains old Polish Pastorales with their tunes; to which are added several popular melodies not intended to be sung in church. Mioduszewski has also published a collection of ancient and modern prayers and songs used in the Roman Catholic Church of Poland (Cracow, 1838), with three supplements (Leipzig, 1842, 1853, 1854).

Again, some European nations possess certain hymns, sung in divine worship, which have become so popular that they may properly be classed with the genuine national music. If we remember that the German citizens, on solemn occasions of the highest import for the Fatherland—such as the conquest of an aggressive enemy, the extermination of a raging epidemic, or other national calamity—assemble in the open place of the town to unite their voices in singing the chorale, "Nun danket alle Gott" (Now thank we all our God), we cannot but regard the song and its impressive performance in a grand unison as truly national to Germany. In fact, not a few of the tunes of the old chorales were originally secular national airs. Every musician knows that in our sacred music we possess many of the most elaborate and most beautiful works of our classical composers. However, in our present research the intrinsic value of the music exclusively, or even pre-eminently, does not concern us; we have to direct our attention to such sacred music only as is stamped with certain characteristics in its construction or performance peculiar to the taste of a certain nation or race. The synagogical music of the Jews affords, in this respect, an excellent example for investigation. Although some of the hymns of the Jews may not date from so high an antiquity as is assigned to them by certain editors of Hebrew sacred songs, there can be no doubt that they are very old, and the manner of performance of them in the synagogue partakes of an oriental character. This circumstance alone would be sufficient to recommend to the student a careful examination of the Jewish music, were it not on account of its associations with the Temple music of the Hebrews at the time of David and Solomon. The published collections of Jewish sacred songs contain usually, amidst a number of tunes composed by the editor or selected by him from modern compositions, a few old standard tunes, which the student has to pick out. In the following books he will find rather more for his purpose than in other publications of the kind:

"Schir Zion; Gottesdienstliche Gesänge der Israeliten," by Salomon Sulzer (Vienna, about 1840; folio). A collection of Hebrew songs, ancient and modern, which are sung in the synagogues at Vienna. The resemblance of the mode of singing, or rather chanting, in the synagogues to the vocal performances of the Persians and other Eastern nations is unmistakable, and shows to some extent how tenaciously the Jews have preserved ancient usages connected with their religious observances.

"Schire Beth Adonai; oder Tempelgesänge für den Gottesdienst der Israeliten," by H. Weintraub (Leipzig, 1859; folio). A large and interesting collection of chants and songs as performed in the synagogues of Königsberg, in Prussia. It contains, besides modern compositions, several melodies which are said to be of high antiquity. H. Weintraub observes that the oldest and most universally used chants in the synagogues are generally in the Phrygian and Mixolydian Modes; and as the popular melodies of the Arabs, Persians, and Turks are frequently based upon similar orders of intervals, he concludes that these chants must have originated in the East. He points this out as affording strong evidence in support of the traditional belief of the Jews that their old chants are the identical ones which were in use at the time when the Israelites sojourned in the Promised Land.

"The Ancient Melodies of the Liturgy of the Spanish and Portuguese Jews; harmonized by Emanuel Aguilar; preceded by an historical essay on the Poets, Poetry, and Melodies of the Sephardic Liturgy," by D. A. De Sola, (London, 1857; royal 8vo). The editor, the Rev. D. A. De Sola, who was minister of the Spanish and Portuguese Congregation of Jews, Bevis Marks, London, says in his interesting historical essay: "A tradition exists with respect to the melody of the 'Blessing of the Priests' that it is identical with that sung in the Temple, where, as it is known, the priestly choirs were daily wont to bless the people agreeably to the command to them in Numbers vi. 22-26. That this tradition is supported by great probability, almost amounting to direct proof, will appear from the following considerations: First, that this duty devolved exclusively on the priests, who were a numerous class, who executed it with religious awe and attention, and who, as a privilege peculiar to themselves, scrupulously transmitted it to their sons. It is, therefore, highly improbable that, on the restoration of public divine service, the priests should have used, or the people would have permitted them to introduce, any other melody except the venerated one of the Temple, especially as the blessing of the people was the only act of administration remaining to the priests after the destruction of the Sanctuary. Secondly, we find that, with slight alteration, this blessing is sung to the same melody in every Sephardic congregation. And though our brethren following the German Liturgy have more than one melody for it, they seem to be of comparatively modern introduction; and one of them, said to be the most ancient, contains unmistakable traces of this, which we must consider to be the original melody."

Even more open to criticism is the bold conjecture of the editor respecting the tune of the " Song of Moses," which is also held to be of very remote origin. The tune is given in the book. De Sola remarks upon it : " According to a very ancient Spanish work, printed, if I recollect rightly, in Portugal, ' Some have affirmed that what we now sing to the " Song of Moses " is the same melody which Miriam and her companions sang.' This legend would not merit any serious consideration here, except that it undoubtedly proves that the knowledge of the origin of the melody was already long lost when the ancient Spanish book was written : and here again the acute remark of Dr. Sachs is applicable, that ' Fable soon occupies itself to speak where history is silent.' It is, therefore, highly probable that this melody belongs to a period anterior to the regular settlement of the Jews in Spain. The general adoption thereof by every congregation of the Sephardic Liturgy furnishes also a strong proof in favour of the high antiquity of its origin."

"Hagadah; oder Erzählung von Israels Auszug aus Egypten, &c.; mit Musikbeilagen," by J. Offenbach (Cologne, 1838 ; 8vo). This curious book, with musical notations of Hebrew songs, contains a solemn narrative of the departure of the Israelites from Egypt, and is intended to be used in the family devotional ceremonies which are observed on the first two evenings of the Matzoth rite, when the Jews eat the unleavened bread called Matzoth, and the "bitter herbs," consisting of a little parsley dipped in vinegar or salt and water. A German translation, printed in juxtaposition to the Hebrew text, enables the uninitiated reader also to comprehend the singular directions, prayers, and reflections in the book, intended to commemorate the great event of the delivery of the Israelites from Egyptian bondage. The editor was the principal singer of the Jewish synagogue at Cologne, and the father of the composer Offenbach, whose flippant operas found recently many admirers, especially in Paris.

"A Selection of Hebrew Melodies, Ancient and Modern, &c.," by T. Nathan. The poetry written expressly for the work by Lord Byron (London, 1824; folio, four vols.). The first edition was published in the year 1815 by Nathan and Braham conjointly.

There are also collections of synagogical songs edited by Salaman and Verrinder (London; oblong 8vo), by A. A. Wolff (Copenhagen, 1839; 8vo), by Emile Jonas (Paris, 1854), by Mayer and Staab (Mayence, 1861; 4to), &c.

As regards the liturgic songs of the Greek Church, a comprehensive collection has been brought out by J. C. N. Chaviara, the principal singer in the Church of the Greeks at Vienna. A revised edition of his work (Vienna, 1859; royal 8vo, six numbers) has the text printed with Roman letters placed under the Greek letters, which may be convenient to some musicians. The melodies are the original Greek ones, but they are harmonised for four voices by B. Randhartinger, the director of the Greek Church music at Vienna. Equally interesting, or perhaps even more so, are the published works of vocal compositions appertaining to the Greek Church of Russia. Take, for instance, the songs arranged for four voices by Peter Tourchannin (St. Petersburg, 1832; folio). The British Museum possesses some old collections of vocal music used in the service of the Greek Church, in 4to, which were printed in Moscow. The circumstance of these works being almost invariably issued with the Russian text only, is to most musicians of Western Europe an obstacle to their familiarising themselves with the compositions, and to their appreciating accurately whatever beauty and impressiveness the music may possess. The same remark applies even more forcibly to the sacred vocal music of nations or races less known in Western Europe than the Russians, as for instance, the Armenians, Copts, Abyssinians, who are Christians; and, still more, to the Pagan sacred music of extra-European nations. A mere notation of such music, without some verbal explanation, is almost as a sealed book. However, we possess, as will presently be shown, treatises which may assist the intelligent inquirer.

MUSICAL INSTRUMENTS.

An acquaintance with the musical instruments of different nations is of great assistance in the study of national music, since the peculiar construction of the instruments enables us in many instances to ascertain with accuracy the characteristic order of intervals, modulations, embellishments, and other such distinctive features prevailing in the music of a nation.

A reliable and really instructive work, intended to give a survey of all the musical instruments in use in different parts of the world, has hitherto not been published. F. J. Fétis evidently appreciated the importance of such an investigation to conjecture from the attention he has given to the subject in his " Résumé philosophique de l'Histoire de la Musique," which prefaces the first edition of his "Biographie universelle des Musiciens " (Paris, 1837), and which he has afterwards incorporated, with additions, in his " Histoire générale de la Musique" (Paris, 1869). Fétis is an intelligent and pleasant writer, and the facility with which he has compiled comprehensive dissertations is as admirable as is his industry. Considering the diversity of the subjects which he has discussed, it is not surprising that some of them should be treated by him rather superficially. At any rate this is the case with national music, which requires more persevering attention than his manifold pursuits permitted him to bestow upon it. His shortcomings are sometimes rather aggravating, since he is apt to express his opinion in a dictatorial manner on questions which have not been positively ascertained by more careful inquirers. To note an instance : In his " Résumé philosophique" he is quite sure that the fiddle-bow originated in Europe ; and in his " Recherches historiques," prefacing his treatise on Antonius Stradiuarius, he is quite sure that it originated in Hindustan. There is nothing reprehensible in a searcher after truth exchanging one theory for another; but opinions which are merely conjectural should be expressed with diffidence: bold assertions which cannot be proved as being indisputable are not likely to satisfy earnest students.

The musical instruments of certain ancient nations have been more carefully investigated than those of most races which are our contemporaries; nor is this surprising, considering how important a part those nations played in the history of the world. The description and illustrations of the musical instruments of the ancient Egyptians, in the works by Lepsius, Rossellini, and Sir Gardner Wilkinson, have proved of much use in the study of musical history; for although these Egyptologists possessed no musical knowledge, the carefulness with which they have sketched and described their discoveries renders their communications reliable and valuable to musicians.

No doubt the taste of a writer who draws attention to a literary work of his own is questionable. There may, however, be instances in which this proceeding is justifiable. Thus "The Music of the Most Ancient Nations, particularly of the Assyrians, Egyptians, and Hebrews, with special reference to recent discoveries in Western Asia and Egypt" (London: J. Murray, 1864; 8vo), claims a passing notice, because it was the first work which contained a circumstantial account, with illustrations, of the interesting Assyrian musical instruments represented on the sculptures which were exhumed, about the middle of the present century, in Western Asia; and also because almost all subsequent writers on Assyrian music have drawn from that book, though not all have had the honesty to point out the source from which they copied their statements. The Assyrian instruments are particularly interesting, since they afford us a hint as to the construction of the Hebrew instruments, of which so much has been written by the commentators on the Bible, but of which, in truth, very little is known. If the exploring expeditions which are engaged in exhuming Hebrew relics in Palestine should succeed in bringing to light sculptures or paintings of musical instruments like those of the Assyrians and ancient

Egyptians, our old treatises on Hebrew music will probably experience some curious rectifications.

As regards the musical instruments of the ancient Greeks and Romans, almost all our standard histories of the art of music contain reliable drawings of them copied from the original illustrations. Nevertheless, extravagant notions as to the characteristics of the Greek instruments are occasionally maintained by some of the numerous writers, dilettanti as well as professional musicians, who have occupied themselves with the subject. To notice an instance—the opinions of Friedrich von Drieberg, in his "Wörterbuch der griechischen Musik" (Berlin, 1835; 4to). This book, which deserves a place in any collection of curiosities in musical literature, contains illustrations of about forty ancient instruments, with explanations more startling than well-founded. The author, who was a chamberlain of the King of Prussia, does not trouble himself to prove his assertions; but he introduces his dictionary with the statement that the subject which he is going to treat has never been properly understood by musical historians, and that all who differ from him are dunces. He is quite sure that the Greeks had a tonal system and scales similar to our own, only more perfect; that they employed harmony as we do; and that their musical instruments were constructed in a high degree of perfection. The circumstance that we do not find any such ingeniously constructed instruments represented on the Greek monuments, he accounts for by the surmise that it was not the custom with the Greek artists to depict other of their instruments than the most primitive and simple ones, the invention of which was assigned to their gods. He gives a detailed description of the hydraulic and pneumatic organs, with diagrams showing their mechanism; and he is quite sure that the hydraulic organ had several stops as well as a keyboard. Nay, the Greeks had, he says, even stringed instruments with a keyboard; for, he argues, it is recorded that they had instruments mounted with forty strings, and how could they play upon any such instrument with so many strings if it was not provided with a keyboard? This example of reasoning of a prejudiced musical historian requires no comment, especially as the unfoundedness of his assertions must be evident to any one acquainted with the descriptions of the Greek instrument given in our standard works on the history of music by Martini, Burney, Forkel, Fétis, Ambros, &c.

As regards the musical instruments of our ancestors during the Middle Ages, representations of them, showing their construction and capabilities, have been published by the Abbot Gerbert ("De Cantu et Musica sacra") and by M. de Coussemaker ("Annales archéologiques"), which are taken from paintings and sculptures, and may be relied upon. It must be borne in mind that the mediæval artists, in depicting a musical instrument in the hands of an angel or some figure of their imagination, not unfrequently adhered as little to nature as do artists in our time. However, with some slight experience, the musical historian has generally no difficulty in discerning the fanciful conceptions.

Turning to the literature on musical instruments of the post-mediæval centuries, we meet with a considerable number of works. The most important ones shall briefly be noticed. Only one of the earliest publications shall be described somewhat more circumstantially, since it may interest the reader to ascertain the plan and form of such an early production.

The book alluded to is written in German, and is entitled "Musica getutscht und ausgezogen durch Sebastianum Virdung" (Basel, 1511; 4to). S. Virdung, who was a priest living in Amberg, Bavaria, states in his dedication of the book to Bishop Wilhelm, in Strasburg, that the publication consists of extracts from a larger work, the printing of which he has been obliged to postpone on account of the great expense it involves. The larger work appears to have remained in manuscript, as nothing further is known about it. The present abridgment is written in the form of a dialogue. After the Dedication, and a Preface which consists chiefly of quotations from the Bible referring to the employment of sacred music, the author gives a wood engraving showing the meeting of two old friends, whose names are Sebastian and Andreas Silvanus. Now follows the instruction, given in dialogue, and commencing as follows:—

"*Andreas.* My dear Herr Bastian! Be thou welcome a thousand times.

"*Sebastian.* Be thanked, my dear friend.

"*Andreas.* And how art thou, my dear Bastian?

"*Sebastian.* Bless thee for the inquiry; I am still pretty well through the mercy of Heaven.

"*Andreas.* Tell me, dear friend, where hast thou been all the time?

"*Sebastian.* I have sought, experienced, and found that for a long time I went a wrong way.

"*Andreas.* What dost thou mean?

"*Sebastian.* I mean, as regards the beautiful, practical, and instrumental Musica.

"*Andreas.* I have been told that thou hast for a long while contemplated to produce something new and singular, but I do not know in what it consists. Therefore, if thou canst spare a little time, I pray thee to show and explain it to me.

"*Sebastian.* I am quite willing to oblige in this, and even in matters of much greater import, in as far as I can do it without disadvantage to myself.

"*Andreas.* Dear friend! I assure thee, in good faith, thou shalt not come to harm by this. Let me see.

"*Sebastian.* It requires much labour and examination; besides, thou dost not understand the German explanations so well as thou understandest Latin poetry. If thou likest to look over the pictures of the instruments, thou art welcome; but to read the whole, this would take thee too long a time.

"*Andreas.* My dear friend, allow then that I survey it briefly.

"*Sebastian.* Very well, take it and inspect it carefully.

"*Andreas.* My good man, thou hast many nice pictures in the book! What is thy object with them?"

After a few more of such introductory sentences, which, no doubt, the author thought flowing and elegant, Sebastian explains the woodcuts. They represent the following instruments:—

Clavicordium. The clavichord. Virdung says, "I believe that the *clavicordium* is the same instrument which Guido Aretinus called *monocordum*, on account of its having had originally but a single string. For a long time it had not more than thirty keys."

Uirginal. An oblong-square spinet; the English *virginal.*

Lyra. The hurdy-gurdy, also called *lyra mendicorum.*

Clavicymbalum. The harpsichord.

Clavicitherium. Of this instrument Virdung remarks: "It is just like the *uirginal*, except that its strings are made of sheep's gut; they are twanged by means of nails and quills. It has only been recently invented, and I have seen only one specimen."

Lauten. Lutes. He mentions four different kinds, mounted with nine, eleven, thirteen, and fourteen strings; and he describes the different parts of the lute, and its tablature.

Grosse Geige. The antiquated large fiddle.

Quintern. The antiquated *quinterna*, twanged with a quill.

Harpffen. Harps. He mentions three kinds, and says that they are usually made in a triangular shape; that the new ones have a greater number of strings than the old ones.

Psalterium. Two kinds, viz., the triangular and the quadrangular.

Hackbrett. The dulcimer.

Kleine Geige. The antiquated small fiddle.

Trumscheit. The marine trumpet.

Schalmey (shalm), *Bombardt, Schwegel, Zwergpfeiff, Flöten, Russpfeiff, Krummhorn, Sensenhorn, Zinken, Platerspiel, Sackpfeiff,* (bagpipe), *Busaun* (trombone), *Feldtrummet* (military trumpet), *Clareta* (small trumpet), *Thurnerhorn, Orgel, Positive, Regale, Cymbals, Glocken* (bells), *Baucken* (*i.e., Pauken*, or kettle-drums), *Ampos vnd Hemmer* (*i.e.*, anvil and hammers). As regards the last-named instrument, the musical reader will probably remember that the sound of the anvil beaten by a blacksmith is said to have suggested to Pythagoras important discoveries in acoustics. However this may be, the anvil has certainly been employed as a musical instrument in several modern operas; for instance, in "Alcidor," by Spontini, and in "Rheingold," by Wagner.

Nay, at the American "International Peace Jubilee" at Boston, in the year 1872, an "Anvil Chorus" was performed with the rhythmical accompaniment of a hundred anvils, which were struck by a hundred Boston firemen.

Ottomarus Luscinius, a German priest, whose proper name was Nachtigall, published in the year 1536, at Strasburg, a little book in Latin, with illustrations of musical instruments, entitled "Musurgia seu Praxis Musicæ." A considerable portion of this work is merely a translation of passages from Virdung's "Musica getutscht und ausgezogen." Sir John Hawkins, in his "General History of Music" (London, 1776; vol. ii., p. 442), gives illustrations of musical instruments copied from the "Musurgia" of Luscinius.

Other noteworthy publications containing descriptions and illustrations of the musical instruments of our forefathers are:—

"Musica instrumentalis," by Martin Agricola (Wittemberg, 1529; sm. 8vo); "De Organographia," by Michael Prætorius (Wolfenbüttel, 1619; 4to); "Harmonie universelle," by F. Marin Mersenne (Paris, 1636; folio); "Musurgia universalis," by Athanasius Kircher (Rome, 1650; folio, two vols.); "Gabinetto armonico pieno d'istromenti sonori," by Filippo Bonanni (Rome, 1722; 4to; second edition, with a French translation, in 1776); "Essai sur la Musique," by Laborde (Paris, 1780; 4to, four vols.); "Musica Mechanica Organoedi," by Jakob Adlung (Berlin, 1768; 4to). The last named is one of the most instructive works on the subject in question; those by Bonanni and Laborde are the least useful.

The more modern treatises on musical instruments may be noticed here with but few words, as they are easily accessible. A treatise by Wilhelm Schneider, entitled "Historisch-technische Beschreibung der musikalischen Instrumente" (Neisse and Leipzig, 1834; 8vo), contains descriptions of instruments without illustrations. On the other hand, a compilation by Welcker von Gontershausen, entitled "Neu-eröffnetes Magazin musikalischer Tonwerkzeuge" (Frankfort, 1855; 8vo), contains many illustrations; however, the explanations are often unsatisfactory. In

France, Le Dulcet, Comte de Pontécoulant, published in the year 1861, in Paris, a work in two volumes entitled "Organographie; essai sur la facture instrumentale," which is an enlarged edition of a former publication by the same author (Paris, 1857). It is well spoken of by F. J. Fétis; but it is already out of print. It hardly deserves the praise bestowed on it by Fétis. The chapter which most inquirers will probably find interesting is that which gives an account of the various inventions of sound-producing means for musical performances which have been patented in France down to the year 1861. The names of German inventors are often vexatiously misspelt, and the names originally given by the inventors to their productions are translated into French, which renders it almost impossible to ascertain the real names.

The fine engravings of musical instruments in the *planches* belonging to the French encyclopædias of the eighteenth century ought to be known to the student.

Attention must also be drawn to the treatises on instrumentation, especially the work by Hector Berlioz, of which an English translation by Mary Cowden Clarke (London: Novello, Ewer and Co., 1856; royal 8vo) deserves to be noticed; likewise "Instrumentation," by Ebenezer Prout (London: Novello, Ewer and Co., 1878). The "Manuel général de Musique militaire," by Georges Kastner (Paris, 1848), contains numerous drawings of military instruments. There are other modern dissertations of this kind which it is unnecessary to point out. Friedrich Zamminer has written a useful work on musical instruments considered in their relations to the law of acoustics, the German title of which is "Die Musik und die musikalischen Instrumente in ihrer Beziehung zu den Gesetzen der Akustik" (Giessen, 1855; 8vo). The book is illustrated with above a hundred woodcuts. The celebrated work on acoustics by H. Helmholtz, "Die Lehre von den Tonempfindungen," should of course not be unknown to the student. An English translation of this work, by A. J. Ellis has been published in London.

Treatises on the history and manufacture of certain musical instruments in common use with European nations, and books of instruction for playing the instruments are likewise noteworthy; however, it will suffice here to mention the fact, since the reader may be supposed to be acquainted with the most important books of this kind. Even a short account of all our own instruments in use at the present day would fill a volume. Hector Berlioz, in his "Treatise on Modern Instrumentation and Orchestration," notices about sixty, and this is not the half of the number extant, if we include the various instruments which have no place in the orchestra, not to speak of the innumerable new inventions employed in military bands. As regards the Hindus, Chinese, and several other Asiatic nations, at least fifty instruments can be assigned to each of them. On the other hand, there are nations which evidently possess not more than half a dozen. If ten only be taken as the average number of instruments for each nation or tribe, and 150 as the number of the nations or tribes which, as has been ascertained, possess instruments of their own, it will be seen that about 1,500 would require to be described in a survey of the musical instruments of all nations.

Fine illustrations of the instruments of the Arabs and the Chinese are given in the treatises by Villoteau and Amiot, which will presently come under notice; and illustrations of Japanese instruments are to be found in Siebold's celebrated work on Japan; but the work does not contain any explanations respecting the instruments. Moreover the student of national music would do well to consult the published catalogues of the collections of musical instruments deposited in public museums. The latest edition of the "Descriptive Catalogue of the Musical Instruments in the South Kensington Museum" (London, 1874), describes 353 instruments, and is illustrated with 143 wood-engravings and six photographs. This edition, which is the second, is preceded by an essay on the history of musical instruments. The first edition appeared in the year 1870. In France an interesting descriptive catalogue of the instruments in the Musée du Conservatoire National de Musique has been compiled by Gustave Chouquet (Paris, 1875). This book unfortunately does not possess any illustrations, which is a drawback to those students who have not the opportunity of visiting the museum and of inspecting the objects described in the book. Fine photographs of a selection of thirty-five specimens from the instruments belonging to the Liceo Comunale di Musica, in Bologna, were made about the year 1872, under the direction of Gaetano Gaspari, the curator of the Museum, and contain some literary explanation printed with them. There seems to be now a prospect that also in this branch of musical art, which has been so long neglected, some progress will be made; at all events, if report may be relied upon, there are now antiquarians in different European countries who have taken it earnestly in hand. G. Nottebohm is said to be occupied with the compilation of a descriptive catalogue of the instruments belonging to the Gesellschaft der Musikfreunde (Society of Lovers of Music), in Vienna; Victor Mahillon is engaged in preparing a similar work for the Museum of the Belgian Conservatoire Royal de Musique at Brussels; Max Freiherr von Branca has made about 500 drawings of instruments deposited in the different Museums at Munich, which he intends to publish as illustrative of the history of instrumental music, with special regard to military bands; C. Södling, in Westervik, Sweden, has been for years occupied in writing a history of Scandinavian music, in which he purposes to give an account, with illustrations, of scarce Swedish and Norwegian instruments, which are sure to be unknown to most musicians; Alexander Kraus, of Florence, has recently formed a comprehensive collection of antiquated and scarce instruments, including Italian specimens of the violin family, obtained by him during his search in Italian towns, and he is engaged in preparing a descriptive catalogue of his acquisitions, which, no doubt, will prove a valuable guide to musical antiquarians. If I venture here to add that I have nearly finished the manuscript of a comprehensive work in which I have endeavoured to give an account of all the musical instruments in the world, as far as I have been able to become acquainted with them, and that the work is illustrated with about 800 drawings of instruments, most of which have hitherto not been mentioned in any musical publication, I run the risk of incurring the censure of some musicians as being actuated by a selfish motive. Reasonable readers will however understand that such a work, the accomplishment of which has required long-continued perseverance, must have been a labour of love and of disinterestedness, as far as personal advantage comes in question; and for such readers only the statement is intended.

TREATISES.

In our survey of the collections of national songs, we have already become acquainted with several treatises which are published as introductory to the collections. It remains now to notice the most important treatises relating to national music which have been brought out independently of any collection. Let us turn first to Asia.

Sir William Jones's essay "On the Musical Modes of the Hindus," written in the year 1784, and subsequently much enlarged by the author, is printed in "Asiatic Researches" (Calcutta, 1792; vol. iii., p. 55); in "Dissertations and Miscellaneous Pieces relating to the History and Antiquities, &c., of Asia" (London, 1796; 8vo, vol. iii.); and in "The Works of Sir William Jones" (London, 1799; 4to, vol. i., p. 413). A German translation of this essay, by F. H. von Dalberg (Erfurt, 1802; 4to), contains some additional accounts respecting the music of uncivilised nations. "An Essay on the Music of Hindustan," by Sir William Ouseley, is printed in "Oriental Collections," &c. (London, 1797; 4to, vol. i., p. 70). Augustus Willard's "Treatise on the Music of Hindustan" (Calcutta, 1834; 8vo), contains many statements respecting the history of music in general which may be supposed to be well-known to any one who intends to study the music of the Hindus. However, among the unnecessary statements the author occasionally and sometimes incidentally mentions facts referring to the popular songs and tunes of Hindustan which deserve the careful attention of the student. The most interesting chapters in the book are those which treat of the *Rags* and *Raginees*, of musical instruments, of vocal compositions, and of the peculiar manners and customs of the Hindus to which allusions are made in their popular songs.

A treatise on Hindu music, written in Bengali, and entitled "Sangeeta Sára," by Khettra Mohana Gosvâmee, has been published in two parts (Calcutta, 1869; 4to).

Attention must also be drawn to the contributions to musical literature, written in Sanskrit and Bengali, by the Rajah Sourindro Mohun Tagore, and published at Calcutta in the years 1870-75. A mere enumeration of the titles of these books and pamphlets, about a dozen in number, would be of little use here, and a description of them would require too much space; besides, it is hardly necessary, since a statement of their contents has been published in the "Annuaire du Conservatoire Royal de Musique de Bruxelles, Ire Année" (Brussels, 1877; 8vo), which is easily obtainable. But it may interest the reader to know that the Rajah Sourindro Mohun Tagore is the President of the Musical Academy of Bengal, in the foundation of which, in the year 1871, he took the initiative. Although this institution is organised upon the model of European Conservatoires, its chief object is to promote the cultivation of Hindu national music.

An elaborate treatise on the music of the Chinese, written by the Jesuit missionary Amiot, and illustrated with fine engravings of musical instruments, forms the sixth volume of " Mémoires concernant l'histoire, les sciences, les arts, les mœurs, les usages, &c., des Chinois, par les Missionnaires de Pékin " (Paris, 1780; 4to). It is rather unfortunate for musical students that some of the most interesting treatises on the art are incorporated in voluminous and expensive publications, and are not procurable separately, except by some chance which rarely occurs. Amiot is said to have sent to Paris several manuscripts of essays on Chinese music, besides that which has been printed. Adrien de la Fage, in his " Histoire générale de la Musique " (Paris, 1844; vol. i., p. 10), states that they are unaccountably lost; and he deplores the loss of Amiot's translation of a treatise on music written by Ly-Koang-ti, a learned Chinese who lived in the eighteenth century. The Abbé Arnaud published an abridgment of this treatise in the "Variétés littéraires, ou Recueil des Pièces tant originales que traduites" (Paris, 1768). Moreover, the treatise was published in a Spanish translation, at Madrid, in the year 1779. Adrien de la Fage doubts this. He says that no one has seen the Spanish translation, and that all his inquiries about it have been unsuccessful. F. J. Fétis is of the same opinion. He says ("Biographie universelle des Musiciens," vol. i., p. 90): "Lichtenthal indique (' Bibliogr. della Musica,' t. iii., p. 43) d'après un article du 'Journal Encyclop.' (Mars, 1780; t. ii., part 3, p. 543) une version espagnole de la traduction française du traité de musique de Ly-Koang-ti, par le père Amiot, sous ce titre ' Memoria sobre la Musica de los Chineses; Madrid, imprinta de Bablo y Texero, 1780.' Malgré ces indications si précises, j'avoué que je doute de l'existence de ce livre; car toutes les recherches que j'ai fait faire à Madrid n'ont pu en faire découvrir un seul exemplaire. La traduction a pu être faite; mais il est vraisemblable qu'elle n'a point paru."

The treatise has, however, been published; and in order to dispel all uncertainty about its existence I shall give a short account of its contents. I obtained in London a copy of "Variedades literarias, ó Coleccion de piezas escogidas de literatura, asi originales, como tracucidas de diversos Idiomas al Frances, pertenecientes á las Artes y Ciencias; por los Señores Arnod y Suard. Traducidas al Castellano por Don Felix Fguia, Presbytero, Teologo, y Examinador del Tribunal de la Nunciatura; Tomo II. En Madrid: en la imprenta de Pedro Marin; Ano de 1779." This book contains, among other essays, the musical one in question. It has the heading: "Traduccion Manuscrita de un libro sobre la Musica de los Chinòs, compuesta por Ly-Koang-ti, Doctor y Miembro del primer Tribunal de Letras, Ministro del Imperio, &c.; adornada de varias reflexiones y notas curiosas." The introductory portion of the treatise evidently emanated from a European pen, perhaps from that of Amiot himself. It points out an apparent or supposed similarity of the Chinese musical system with that of the ancient Egyptians and that of Pythagoras. We are told of the miraculous power attributed to music by the ancient Chinese, and of the wonderful effect of the instrument *Kin*, mounted with silken strings, which in ancient time must have been a sacred instrument, for, we are told, it was never played unless incense was burned during its performance. The author maintains that the character of the Chinese music has experienced in the course of time fewer modifications than have the notions of the Chinese about the art. He records the unsuccessful attempts of the Emperor Kang-hi to introduce into China the European music, with which he had in some measure become acquainted through the Jesuit missionaries; and the author believes that the organ of hearing of the Chinese is constructed somewhat differently from that of the Europeans; this accounts, in his opinion, for their peculiar musical taste. Howbeit, the Emperor Kang-hi soon became convinced that, though he had the power of deciding on the life or death of his subjects, he could not alter their music. The author has much to say respecting ths different kinds of musical performances which formerly were observed at the Court and on certain solemn popular celebrations. He records the construction of improved instruments during the reign of the Emperor Kang-hi, in the latter half of the seventeenth century; however, he adds that the new instruments were made exactly after the pattern of the old ones used at the Imperial Court; the improvements must therefore have been but slight. The subsequent portion of the treatise refers mostly to the history of the art, and to religious and other ceremonies with musical performances. Particularly interesting is the account of the method used by the Chinese music-masters in teaching the signs for reading their music, and suchlike elementary knowledge. This subject would, however, take too much space to discuss here; nor does it come strictly within the scope of the present survey. Sufficient has probably been said to give the reader a correct idea of the treatise under consideration, which occupies about sixty pages in the small octavo volume in which it is printed.

The same volume contains another curious translation, entitled " Memoria sobre los Bayles de los Chinos, sacada de una traduccion manuscrita di algunas obras de Confucio," which refers almost exclusively to the dances of the Chinese, the musical performances accompanying them being referred to only incidentally.

The music of no other Asiatic race has been so carefully investigated by Europeans as that of the Arabs. Among the treatises giving information on the musical system and instruments of the Arabs may be specified :—

" Die Musik der Araber, nach Originalquellen dargestellt, von R. G. Kiesewetter " (Leipzig, 1842 ; 4to).

" Esquisse historique de la Musique Arabe, par Alexandre Christianowitsch " (Cologne, 1863 ; folio).

" La Musique Arabe, ses rapports avec la Musique Grecque et le Chant Grégorien, par F. Salvador Daniel " (Algiers, 1863 ; 8vo).

An instructive chapter on the songs and musical instruments of the Arab-Egyptians is to be found in " An Account of the Manners and Customs of the Modern Egyptians," by E. W. Lane. The first edition of this work appeared in London in the year 1836, and about half a dozen editions of it have subsequently been brought out.

By far the most valuable dissertation on the music of the Arabs is the work by G. A. Villoteau, which forms part of the large and costly publication entitled " Description de l'Egypte, ou Recueil des Observations et des Recherches qui ont été faites en Egypte pendant l'expédition de l'armée française " (Paris, 1809 ; second edition, Paris, 1823). Villoteau's carefully written dissertation is enhanced by the addition of three beautiful plates in folio, showing the described instruments with the peculiar construction of their different portions. Here again the musical student has perhaps to deplore that such interesting information should be almost hidden from him by being incorporated in an expensive work amounting to above twenty volumes. True, several subsequent musical writers of inexpensive books have used much of the information given by Villoteau; but it is always preferable for the student to refer to the original source from which the compilers have drawn.

This remark leads to the expression of a wish wherein the reader will probably likewise join. It is a well-known fact that the more civilised Asiatic nations possess treatises on music. Oriental scholars mention several of the Hindus. Amiot, in his work before cited, gives a list of about seventy by Chinese authors. The Japanese, it may be supposed, are in this respect not behind the Chinese, considering the natural intelligence and inquisitiveness of the former people. As regards the Arabs and the Persians, the names of a number of authors on music are known, and the titles of many treatises. Occasionally a translation into a European language has been attempted, such as, for instance, the English translation published by Eli Smith in the "Journal of the American Oriental Society" (Boston, 1749; vol. i.), which is chiefly derived from a treatise by Mikhâil Meshâkah of Damascus.

.There are considerable difficulties in producing a correct and useful translation of such a work. The translator must not only be thoroughly acquainted with the language in which it is written; he must also be an experienced musician well-informed in our own music, and familiar with the characteristics of the foreign music on which the work treats; he must especially be conversant with the exact meaning of the technical terms used by the author. Where these necessary qualifications are combined in the translator, interesting information might be obtained, particularly from some of the old Arabic treatises, which would probably throw light upon certain obscure questions relating to the history of our own art.

The earliest Arabic writer on music was, as far as is known, the learned El-Kindi, who lived about the middle of the ninth century of our era. There is, however, a treatise on music written by the famous Al-Farabi, of which a faithful translation would be perhaps even more desirable. Al-Farabi wrote his treatise about the year 900 of our Christian era. Three manuscript copies of it are known to be extant. One of these, of which Mariano Soriano Fuertes has published extracts translated into Spanish, is in the Escurial; another is in the Library at Leyden; and a third, which is said to be a particularly fine and clearly written manuscript, is in the Ambrosian Library at Milan. With these sources at his command it would no doubt be possible to a really musical Oriental scholar to produce a valuable rendering in English German, or French, with a fac-simile reproduction of the original drawings of the musical instruments with which the treatise is said to be illustrated.

It is well known that some of the old Arabic, Persian,

Hindu, and Chinese musical theorists exhibit speculations of their own which were not in agreement with the musical systems popular at the time when the theorists wrote. Suggestive though these speculations may be, translations of them are likely to prove less instructive than translations of treatises which explain the music as it actually was or is in practical use.

This may be the place to draw attention to a curious dissertation on the Eastern origin of the national music of the Scotch, written in German, and entitled " Erste Wanderung der ältesten Tonkunst, &c., von G. W. Fink" (Essen, 1831; sm. 8vo). The aim of the author is to prove that the music of the Celtic race was originally derived from Asia, and that its original characteristics were preserved more intact in Scotland than in any other European districts owing to the isolated position of that country, and to similar circumstances. Twenty-four years before the publication of Fink's interesting book, John Gunn, a Scotch musician, had already given, at the end of his treatise entitled "An Historical Enquiry respecting the Performance on the Harp in the Highlands of Scotland," &c. (Edinburgh, 1807; 4to), a prospectus of "An Enquiry into the Antiquity of the Harp, and into the Oriental Extraction and Ancient History of the Caledonian Scots, demonstrating from the language, ancient religion, superstitious rites, their kalendar and festivals, their remarkable traditions, manners and customs, and from other documents and monuments still existing in Asia, France, Great Britian, and Ireland, that they brought the harp, together with other arts of civilized life, from Armenia and the western coast of Asia into the southern parts of England, prior to the era at which our writers commence the history of Great Britain," &c. This contemplated work has never been published, which is the less to be deplored since—to judge from the circumstantial prospectus, of which the commencement only is here quoted—the author proves himself too superficially acquainted with Oriental music for the successful execution of his projected task. G. W. Fink was evidently far better prepared for engaging in the same inquiry. Perhaps he had seen the prospectus issued by

J. Gunn, and it suggested to him to investigate the questions raised by the Scotchman. However this may be, he would not have laid so much stress upon the similarity of the musical scale without the intervals of the fourth and seventh, traceable in the music of the Scotch and of the Chinese, had he been aware of its existence in the music of several nations in different parts of the world, of which there appears not to be the slightest probability that they borrowed it from each other. In fact, this peculiar order of intervals, which is now known as the pentatonic scale, may not improperly be regarded as the most natural musical scale, because evidences are not wanting which show that it naturally suggests itself to people whose music is in its infancy; and because it has often been observed that, even in European countries where the diatonic scale prevails, little children in their first attempts to sing this series of intervals are apt to omit the two semitones and to produce the pentatonic series. At any rate, unbiassed investigators must admit that the pentatonic scale is more simple, more impressive, and easier to sing than the diatonic scale; and these qualifications perhaps sufficiently account for its frequent occurrence in the tunes of uncivilised nations or tribes widely separated and having little or no affinity with each other. Although the subject is suggestive and very important to the student of national music, a further discussion of it would be out of place in the present essay. I shall, therefore, restrict myself to citing only one example in confirmation of the opinion expressed.

The reader will probably remember the so-called Jubilee Singers—emancipated negro-slaves from the United States of North America, who visited Europe for the purpose of giving concerts to obtain funds for the establishment of a college at Nashville, in Tennessee, for the higher education of the freed negroes. In "The Story of the Jubilee Singers, with their Songs" (London: Hodder and Stoughton, 1876; 8vo, fourth edition), are given above a hundred airs in notation, with some curious statements respecting their origin and performance, communicated by T. F. Seward. He remarks: "Their origin is unique. They are never composed after the manner of ordinary music, but spring into life, ready made, from the white heat of religious fervour during some protracted meeting in church or camp. They come from no musical cultivation whatever, but are the simple, ecstatic utterances of wholly untutored minds. From so unpromising a source we could reasonably expect only such a mass of crudities as would be unendurable to the cultivated ear. On the contrary, however, the cultivated listener confesses to a new charm, and to a power never before felt, at least in its kind." Having pointed out as a noticeable feature of the airs the rare occurrence of triple time, or three-part measure, the cause of which he assigns to the habit which these negroes have of beating the foot and swaying the body while singing —motions which are in even measure and in regular time—he remarks: "It is a coincidence worthy of note that more than half the melodies in this collection are in the same scale as that in which Scottish music is written; that is, with the fourth and seventh tones omitted. The fact that the music of the ancient Greeks is also said to have been written in this scale suggests an interesting inquiry as to whether it may not be a peculiar language of nature, or a simpler alphabet than the ordinary diatonic scale, in which the uncultivated mind finds its easiest expression."

The Germans possess a considerable number of treatises on music translated from foreign languages. The English possess but few such publications, their translations of foreign works on music being mostly from productions of a rather gossiping kind. There are, however, indications of an increasing demand in England for really instructive works; indeed, this must be the natural consequence of the greatly increasing extent to which the musical art has been practically cultivated in England since about the middle of the present century. The following books are, almost all of them, either in English, in French, or in German—languages which may be supposed to be known to many intelligent musicians. It would probably be of but little use here to enumerate the treatises written in other than those languages.

"Ueber die Musik der neuern Griechen," by R. G. Kiesewetter (Leipzig, 1838; 4to). The student will find interesting specimens of tunes of the modern Greeks, Turks, and Wallachians, in "Geschichte des transalpinischen Daciens," by F. J. Sulzer (Vienna, 1781; 8vo, three vols.). Chrysanthos has published two works on the music of the modern Greeks, which are written in the Greek language. The first of these works is an "Introduction to the Theory and Praxis of the Greek Church music." It was neatly printed by Rignoux in Paris, in the year 1821, and was intended for publication in Constantinople. The other is a similar work, but larger, and not so well brought out; it was printed, in the year 1832, by Michael Weiss, in Trieste.

"Histoire de la Musique en Russie. Première Partie: Musique Sacrée, suivie d'un Choix de Morceaux de Chants d'Eglise anciens et modernes," par le Prince Nicolas Youssoupoff (Paris, 1862; royal 8vo). The author's intention to publish, in a second volume, a treatise on the secular national songs of Russia has not yet been carried out. The student would do well to consult "Dissertations sur les Antiquités de Russie, contenant l'ancienne mythologie, les rites payens, les fêtes sacrées, les jeux, les oracles, l'ancienne musique, les instrumens de musique villageoise, les coutumes, les cérémonies, l'habillement, les divertissemens de village, les mariages, les funérailles, l'hospitalité nationale, les repas, &c., des Russes, comparés avec les mêmes objets chez les Anciens, et particulièrement chez les Grecs; par Matthieu Guthrie" (St. Petersburg, 1795; 8vo). An elaborate treatise on Russian Church music, written by Razumoffsky, in Russian, and containing many curious notations with explanations, has been issued in two volumes (Moscow, 1867 and 1869; 8vo).

A treatise on Russian Church Songs, written in German, by Alexis von Lwoff, is entitled "Ueber den Freien-Rhythmus des altrussischen Kirchengesangs" (St. Petersburg, 1859; royal 8vo). A. von Lwoff is the composer of the well-known Russian National Anthem, which resembles the "Sicilian Mariners' Hymn."

"Entstehung, Fortgang, und jetzige Beschaffenheit der Russischen Jagdmusik, von J. C. Hinrichs" (St. Petersburg, 1796; 4to). An account of the so-called Russian Horn Band, in which each performer has only a single tone; with illustrations and specimens of the peculiar notation contrived for insuring that each player falls in with his note at the right moment. The inventor of the Russian Horn Band, Johann Anton Maresch, was born in the year 1719 in Bohemia, and migrated in the year 1748 to St. Petersburg.

"Beiträge zur Kenntniss der Slavischen Volkspoesie, von F. v. Miklosich" (Vienna, 1870; folio). "Historical View of the Languages and Literature of the Slavic Nations, with a Sketch of their Popular Poetry," by Talvj (New York, 1850; 8vo).

"Des Bohémiens et de leur Musique en Hongrie, par F. Liszt" (Paris, 1859; small 8vo). A German translation of the same. "Die Zigeuner und ihre Musik in Ungarn, deutsch bearbeitet von Peter Cornelius" (Pesth, 1861; 8vo). The style of this book is rather bombastic, and the author states but few instructive facts, although he displays much sentiment respecting the music of the gipsies.

"Music and the Anglo-Saxons; being some account of the Anglo-Saxon Orchestra; with remarks on the Church Music of the Nineteenth Century," by F. D. Wackerbarth (London, 1837; 8vo). This book is noticed here only on account of the interesting subject on which it professes to treat. It is an unsatisfactory compilation, and its title is the best part of the book.

"Musical Memoirs of Scotland, with historical annotations and numerous illustrative plates," by Sir John Graham Dalyell (Edinburgh, T. G. Stevenson, 1749; 4to). The value of this book, which is replete with extraneous matter, consists in the interesting illustrations of ancient musical instruments, taken from old sculptures and paintings extant in Scotland and England.

"Die Minnesänger und Liederdichter des 12, 13, und 14 Jahrhunderts, von F. H. Hagen" (Leipzig, 1838; 4to, 3 vols.); with specimens of mediæval songs in notation.

"Ueber die Lais, Sequencen und Leiche; ein Beitrag zur Geschichte der rhythmischen Formen und Singweisen der Volkslieder und der volksmässigen Kirchen—und Kunstlieder im Mittelalter," von Ferdinand Wolf (Heidelberg, 1841; 8vo);

with eight fac-similes and nine plates of musical notation. An account of the national songs of the Middle Ages will be found in "Histoire de l'Harmonie au Moyen Age, par E. de Coussemaker" (Paris, 1852; 4to). The student will do well to consult "The Lays of the Minnesingers, or German Troubadours of the twelfth and thirteenth centuries; illustrated by specimens of the contemporary lyric poetry of Provence and other parts of Europe; with historical and critical notices, and engravings from the MS. of the Minnesingers in the King's Library at Paris, and from other sources" (London, 1825; 8vo). The annotations are by Edgar Taylor.

"Altcechische Leiche, Lieder, und Sprüche des XIV. und XV. Jahrhunderts; mit einer Einleitung und Anmerkungen, von Julius Feifalik" (Vienna, 1862; 8vo); "Volksschauspiele aus Mähren; mit Anhängen: 1, Sterndreherlieder; 2, Weihnachtslieder; 3, De Sancta Dorothea, Passional, 1495: und einem Nachtrage, gesammelt und herausgegeben von Julius Feifalik" (Olmütz, 1864; 8vo).

"On Purity in Musical Art, by Anton Friedrich Justus Thibaut (Heidelberg, 1825), translated from the German by W. H. Gladstone" (London, John Murray, 1877; sm. 8vo). The German title of this book is "Ueber Reinheit der Tonkunst." The first edition was published in the year 1825, at Heidelberg, without the name of the author. The little book, written with much spirit, and entirely free from the pedantry so usual in musical treatises, produced sensation among the German musicians and lovers of the art. The second edition (Heidelberg, 1826) contains several additions, and a portrait of Palestrina. A third edition, edited by K. Bähr, appeared in 1851, and a fourth in 1875. Thibaut was a professor of law at Heidelberg, and an ardent admirer of the old Italian and Flemish church composers. His book is mentioned here especially on account of an interesting essay on National Songs which it contains.

VARIOUS SOURCES.

SOME interesting information concerning the music of uncivilised nations or tribes is occasionally to be found in books of travel. It is, however, a laborious task for the inquiring musician to pick out the information from those books; he may peruse a comprehensive journal without meeting with a single statement of use for his purpose; or, should he find one which appears to him instructive, there is every probability that it is expressed in words so vague and indistinct as to be useless. Nay, among the published journals of English travellers there are not a few in which the musical performances of foreign nations, if they are alluded to at all, are almost sure to be spoken of disparagingly, and perhaps with an apology for noticing a subject so insignificant. Most travellers are too little acquainted with music to be able to discern what is noteworthy; besides, mere travelling does not make any one a keen observer. A well-prepared person, in walking for half an hour in his garden, may discover more interesting facts than a rambler during a half-year's walk in a distant land. The statements relating to the music of foreign nations given by travellers who possess but slight musical knowledge, ought generally to be received with caution. These informants are apt to employ technical terms and expressions supposed by them to be artistic, which are often incorrect and misleading. Nay, sometimes they express just the contrary of what they intend to say. For instance, the natives of a country are stated to have sung in "pleasant harmony," when it is evident that they have sung an air in unison. A performance is said to have been "very harmonious," when the music pleased our informant; did it appear rather sad to him, he records that it was in a minor key; and if there was something peculiar in the performance which he cannot explain, he terms it "a wild cadence." A stringed instrument having a neck is almost sure to be called "a sort of guitar;" and if it happens to be mounted with four strings, we have perhaps an allusion to the Greek tetrachord, with a quotation from Burney's "History of Music." A wind-instrument with finger-holes is "a flute," no matter whether it is constructed with a single reed in the mouth-hole, like the clarionet, with a double reed, like the hautboy, or with a plug, like the flageolet. A wooden harmonicon, like the marimba or balafo of the negroes, is "a piano;" and when we are told that a native minstrel executed with admirable skill his plaintive national tunes on "a mouth-organ," we are left in uncertainty as to whether the instrument was a Jew's harp or a pandean pipe like the Hebrew ugab. However, it is hardly necessary to show that most of the musical information offered in English books of travel is useless, since the student has probably ascertained this already from experience.

Neither is it surprising that the published journals of missionaries should generally be unsatisfactory for useful musical information, considering how imperfectly the mind of many of these writers has been cultivated for observation, discernment, and application. It was very different with the Jesuit missionaries during the eighteenth century. Their scientific attainments enabled them to investigate and describe accurately the usages, sentiments, and accomplishments of the nations which they visited. The result has been that some of their communications are still highly appreciated, and justly so.

On the other hand, the musical student owes a debt of gratitude to modern travellers for having brought over to England specimens of musical instruments from different remote parts of the world. He has it thus in his power to examine minutely many of the curious contrivances which he finds alluded to in books of travel, and of the real construction of which it would be impossible for him to form an idea from those books. Many of the musical instruments brought to Europe are deposited in public museums or in private collections. With those which are constructed with sonorous slabs of wood or metal, with wind-instruments having finger-holes, and with wind-instruments constructed of a number of tubes, as is the case with the pandean pipe, the musician has generally no difficulty in ascertaining the series of tones producible on the instruments. This is also in some degree possible with stringed instruments provided with frets; however, the frets, which usually consist of cords wound round the neck, are liable to become disarranged in the course of time, and not much reliance can therefore be placed on the positions of the frets of most of the stringed instruments brought from distant countries, and often roughly handled. As regards the manner of playing the instruments, and their combination in musical performances, the student has of course to consult the statements of witnesses.

Among the various sources for information on the music of uncivilised and semi-civilised nations, we must not leave unnoticed the periodical publications of Geographical and Anthropological Societies; and especially certain English works treating on the social life, manners and customs, legends, and fairy-tales of some particular foreign nation. I have already had occasion in the present survey to draw attention to these noteworthy sources; a few books of the kind, concerning extra-European nations, may however be pointed out here by way of example, to guide the inquirer on the right track.

"The Chinese as they are; their moral, social, and literary character; a new analysis of the language, with succinct views of their principal arts and sciences;" by G. Tradescant Lay (London, 1841; 8vo), contains a chapter on the music of the Chinese, with illustrations of instruments. A dissertation on the same subject, by the same author, has been published in "The Chinese Repository" (Canton, 1840), p. 38.

"A Narrative of a Mission sent by the Governor-General of India to the Court of Ava" (London, 1858; 4to), contains much information respecting the music and musical instruments of the Burmese.

"Zeitschrift der deutschen morgenländischen Gesellschaft" (Leipzig, 1851; vol. v.), contains an account of the music of the Armenians, by Petermann.

"Polynesian Mythology and Ancient Traditional History of the New Zealand Race," by Sir George Grey (London, 1855; 8vo), contains an essay on the native songs of New Zealand, by J. A. Davies.

"Polynesian Researches," by William Ellis (London, 1829; 8vo, two vols.), contains an account of the music and musical instruments of the South Sea Islanders.

"An Account of the Natives of the Tonga Islands, in the South Pacific Ocean; compiled and arranged from the extensive communications of Mr. William Mariner, several years resident in those islands;" by John Martin (London, 1817; 8vo, two vols.). This interesting work, of which a second edition, "with an original Grammar and Vocabulary of their Language," appeared in 1818, contains much information respecting the songs and dances of the Tonga Islanders, with tunes in notation.

Likewise, in the musical journals, of which almost every European country possesses some periodical publications, interesting communications relating to national music are occasionally to be met with. Especially the *Allgemeine Musikalische Zeitung*, which was founded in the year 1798 by F. J. Rochlitz, edited from 1827 to 1841 by G. W. Fink, and subsequently by other distinguished musical *savants* (Leipzig: Breitkopf und Härtel; 4to), ought to be consulted; and this the student may accomplish with all the greater facility since a compiled index of the contents of the voluminous publication has been issued.

Now, in glancing over the numerous titles of collections of songs with their tunes, and of treatises, given in the present survey, the student will probably surmise that the subject has been so fully investigated as to be nearly exhausted. But a little further consideration must soon convince him that this is far from being the case. True, some important progress has been made during the last fifty years; the most valuable books mentioned in our survey have, with a few exceptions, been published in the present century. However, only a few countries have hitherto been carefully explored; the great majority remain even now to the musical inquirer a sealed book. Nay, even in countries where so many searches have been made that it might be thought no stone had been left unturned, unexpected finds to a considerable amount are not unfrequently brought to light. To note an instance of recent occurrence. There are, as we have seen, numerous published collections of Scotch national songs. Many of the editors of these collections did not gather the airs of the songs from oral communication, but merely copied them, or at least the greater number of them, from previous books. We meet therefore with certain favourite tunes over and over again in many books. Nevertheless the number of different tunes is very great; we could hardly expect to find it still considerably increased by new searches among the country-people. However, a recent publication, entitled " Traditional Ballad Airs, procured in the Counties of Aberdeen, Banff, and Moray," edited by W. Christie (Edinburgh: Edmonston and Douglas), suggests that even in Scotland an efficient and discerning musical antiquarian would find his pursuit rewarded by new acquisitions.

In Wales, at all events in the northern district of the principality, which Edward Jones ransacked already nearly a hundred years ago, a search after old national tunes may appear even less likely to yield an interesting result than in other parts of the British Island. Still, also here, I cannot help thinking, valuable additions to the Welsh airs which have been published might be obtained. In support of this opinion I shall insert here a Welsh dance-tune which I heard played, about ten years ago, by an old blind harper in Llangollen. He called it "Dixon's Hornpipe," and played it, at my request for old Welsh tunes, with some others which were well-known ones. The originality and boldness of modulation which characterise the tune induced me to commit it at once to paper. Having it afterwards again played by the old blind minstrel, I was enabled to render as faithfully as possible not only the melody but likewise the peculiar treatment of the harmonious accompaniment. To me this spirited tune appears as fine as any of the finest Welsh tunes in popular favour; but, as I may in this case perhaps be a biassed judge, I would rather leave it to the reader to form his own opinion. I do not fear his judgment, provided he does not pronounce it before he has fully imbibed the characteristics of the music. This he will best achieve by playing it as it is marked, "*con spirito:*"—

A Welsh Hornpipe.

If a foreigner, during a night's stay in a much-frequented Welsh town, can pick up a Welsh tune which has never been printed, how much more easy must it be for a native musician, who is familiar with the language and usages of the people! It is with an especial object that I submit this remark to the consideration of English musicians. Pianoforte teachers, organists, and other musical professors living in the provincial towns, must often have excellent opportunities of collecting airs fron the lips of the peasantry. All that is required is that they take real interest in the pursuit, not engaging in it as a troublesome business, but as a labour of love. In Cornwall it would probably be possible to collect in a short time a number of tunes which are not to be found in any book. Indications of their existence are not wanting. For instance, Cyrus Redding, in his "Illustrated Itinerary of the County of Cornwall" (London, 1842), gives a notation of an old air, called *Fadé*, which the Cornish people sing on May-day, and which is also used by them as a dance-tune. In Northumberland, and in other Northern districts of England, probably tunes somewhat resembling those of the south of Scotland, might be obtained. It certainly appears singular that the English musicians should have neglected to investigate the national songs of the different provinces of their country, while much has been done by collectors in almost every other European country. True, many of the intelligent musicians in England are foreigners, who cannot be expected to occupy themselves with collecting the songs of the English peasantry; neither would they be well qualified for the task, however much they might be inclined to give their attention to it. But surely there are English musicians in London and in the large provincial towns who might achieve good results if they would spend their autumnal holidays in some rural district of the country, associate with the villagers, and listen to their songs. What change can be more desirable for a professional man, who during the greater part of his engagements moves in the fashionable circles of society, and is compelled to inhale the impure air of the concert-room—what can be more beneficial to him than an occasional abode among the peasantry in a village, where the pure and invigorating air, and the beautiful scenery, invite to rambles in the fields and woods, and chase away those morbid feelings and crazy notions which very likely have taken possession of the drawing-room musician?

About a century ago there were still, in many European countries, minstrels, or bards, who preserved traditionally the poetry and music of the people. This class of musicians is now gradually becoming extinct, and with it some of the old national musical instruments. In Esthonia, for instance, the last minstrel who perambulated from village to village to play to the peasants their old tunes on the *kantele*, the old national musical instrument of the Finns, died in the year 1812, and the *kantele* was, so to say, buried with him. In the Ukraine, which, as regards national tunes, is perhaps the most fertile district of Russia, the last popular minstrel of renown who played upon the *bandura*, a stringed instrument of the lute kind which is now seldom heard in the Ukraine, was still alive some years ago, an old man devoid of sight, whose name was Ostap Veresai. Like most of the old minstrels or bards, he was a living depository of old national songs. His fame spread so far throughout the Ukraine that a biographical notice of him, written by A. A. Rusof, has recently been published in Kief. The book in which it is printed is entitled "Kobzar Ostap Veresai," and contains, besides the biographical notice, an article on the songs and musical performances of Ostap Veresai, written by N. V. Lisenko; and a number of his musical effusions given in notation. In Little Russia, the minstrel and singer is called *kobzar* or *bandurista*, from his accompanying his voice on the *kobza* or *bandura*.

From such men it would have been comparatively easy to obtain collections of national airs; but this opportunity has generally been lost, because, at the time when the minstrels flourished, but little value was placed upon such relics by educated listeners, who alone were able to commit the music to notation.

At the present day, it seems, musical lectures will in some respects take the place of these minstrels. However, in order really to promote this interesting branch of the musical art, a more thorough preparation is required than appears to have been thought necessary by most of our lecturers. They might take example from the useful scientific lectures given by scholars who have fully mastered the subject which they discuss. Granted that some gossip on national music, interspersed with some singing of popular airs, and wound up with a stirring appeal to the patriotism of the audience, may prove a pleasant evening entertainment, even for unmusical people, it can be of no real use for the art. Some sentimental talk about the lofty mountains and glorious old castles of the country which shall never crumble into dust may heighten the effect of the musical performances, and the emphatic exclamation that "Britons never shall be slaves" is likely to be applauded with enthusiasm, perhaps most vociferously by those of the audience who are the greatest slaves to their prejudices and passions. Of course, not all our musical lectures exhibit so low a taste; praiseworthy exceptions could be cited. Howbeit, as lectures on national music are seldom printed, it would scarcely be worth while to dwell on this subject of musical literature, were it not that the idea of instructing the people by entertaining lectures is excellent and deserving of every encouragement.

A common defect in discourses on national music is that certain peculiarities which are observed in the music of a nation are represented as appertaining exclusively to that nation, and as constituting the characteristic features of the music of that particular nation, whereas in reality they are traceable in the music of various nations.

In short, musicians who intend to discourse upon this subject would do well to study it earnestly, and to extend their investigation to the music of different countries, instead of confining it to the music of the country on which they propose to instruct others. The present essay may be of assistance to them inasmuch as it points out the various sources of information. I am aware that it is but an imperfect attempt; my consolation must be that there will come other students who will carry it on to greater perfection than, with the limited means at present available, it has been in my power to attain.

INDEX.

	PAGE
ABRAHAMSON, his Danish ballads	8
ACCOMPANIMENTS to national airs	6
ACHAZEL, his songs of Carniola	13
ADLUNG, on instruments	76
AFZELIUS, his Swedish songs	8
AGRICOLA, on instruments	76
AGUILAR, his Hebrew melodies	66
AHLSTRÖM, his Swedish airs	8
AIRS Suisses	21
AL-FARABI, Arabic author	86
ALGERIA, airs of	40
ALLGEMEINE Musikalische Zeitung	96
AMIOT, on Chinese music	78, 82
AMMERBACH, his organ-music	58
ANGLO-SAXON music	91
ANTHOLOGIE Françoise	20
ARABS, their musical treatises	85
ARABS, their songs	38, 40, 48
ARMENIAN songs	51, 69, 95
ARWIDSSON, his Swedish songs	8
ASSYRIAN instruments	71
AUSTRIA, songs of	22
BALLAD and song	53
BALLARD, his French songs	20
BANDURA, instrument	100
BARDALE, a collection of songs	7
BARDS	100
BARDS, Irish	28
BARDS, Welsh	29
BASQUES, their songs	19
BASSE-DANSSEN, Dutch	57
BAUMSTARK and Waldbrühl, their Bardale	7
BAVARIA, songs of	22
BECKER, his German songs	23
BECKER, his Hausmusik	58
BELGIUM, songs of	24
BERGGREEN, his collection of songs	7
BERLIOZ, on Instrumentation	77
BIRD, his Hindu airs	39
BOHEMIA, dances of	54, 60
BOHEMIA, songs of	12, 48, 50, 92
BOLERO, Spain	18, 60
BONANNI, on instruments	76
BOSNIA, songs of	13
BOURGAULT-DUCOUDRAY, his Greek songs	17
BOWRING, Sir John, his national poetry	50
BRAGA, a collection of songs	7
BRAZIL, songs of	43
BRITTANY, songs of	20
BUGGE, his Norwegian songs	8
BUJEAUD, his French songs	19
BULGARIA, poetry of	46
BUNTING, his Irish songs	27
BURMAH, music of	95
BÜSCHING and Hagen, their German songs	22
CAMPHUYSEN, his Dutch songs	24
CANADIAN songs	40
CANTICA Spiritualia	63
CARNIOLA, songs of	13
CARINTHIA, songs of	23
CAROLAN, his Irish melodies	27
CATALOGUES, musical	78, 79
CHAMBERS, his Scotch songs	26
CHAMPFLEURY, his French songs	19
CHANTS de Voyageur	40
CHAPPELL, his English songs	34
CHAVIARA, his songs of the Greek Church	68
CHINA, songs of	49
CHINESE airs	40
CHINESE instruments	95
CHINESE treatise on music	82
CHODZKO, his Persian poetry	40
CHORALE, Germany	65
CHRISTIANOWITCH, on the music of the Arabs	85
CHRISTIE, his Scotch songs	97
CHRISTMAS Carols	63
CHRYSANTHOS, on Greek Church music	90

INDEX.

	PAGE
CLARKE, on the National Anthem	35
CLASING, his Brazilian airs	43
CLEMENTI, his national tunes	7
COLLAN, his Finnish songs	13
COLLECTIONS of national songs	6
CORNWALL, tunes of	99
COUSSEMAKER, his Flemish songs	24
COUSSEMAKER, on mediæval music	92
CRACOW, songs of	11
CROBATIANS, their songs	11
CROTCH, his national tunes	7
CZECHS, their songs	12
CZERWINSKI, on dancing	62
DAINOS, Lithuanian songs	14
DALBERG, his publication	81
DALMATIA, poetry of	46
DALYELL, Sir J., on Scotch music	91
DANCES, Bohemian	54, 60
DANCES, Chinese	84
DANCE-TUNES	54
DANCE-TUNES, Dutch	36, 56
DANCE-TUNES, German	57
DANCING-MASTER, English	55
DANIEL, his songs of Tunis	40
DANIEL, on the music of the Arabs	85
DANSKE Viser fra Middelalderen	8
DAUNEY, on Scotch music	26
DAVIES, on the songs of the Maories	96
DENMARK, poetry of	45, 46, 50
DENMARK, songs of	8
DERVISHES, their tunes	16
DE SOLA, his Hebrew songs	66
DE VIGNOLES and Du Bois, their Freemasons' songs	35
DITFURTH, his Bavarian songs	22
DIXON's hornpipe	97
DOINE, songs of Roumania	50
DOPPELMAIR, his Russian songs	10
DRIEBERG, on the music of ancient Greece	72
D'URFEY, his Wit and Mirth	33
DUTCH dance-tunes	36, 56
DUTCH songs	24, 35
DYBECK, his Swedish tunes	8
EGYPT, ancient, intruments of	71

	PAGE
EGYPT, modern, instruments of	85
EGYPT, songs of	38
EL-KINDI, Arabic author	86
ELLIS, his Polynesian Researches	96
ENGLAND, dances of	55
ENGLAND, poetry of	52
ENGLAND, songs of	32
ERBEN, his songs of Bohemia	12
ERK, his songs of Germany	22
ESSAYS, musical	9, 81
ESTHONIA, poetry of	48
ESTHONIAN minstrel	100
FANDANGO, Spanish dance	18, 61
FAROE Isles, poetry of the	45, 47
FATHER Smith	59
FEIFALIK, on the songs of Bohemia	92
FÉTIS, on Chinese music	83
FÉTIS, on musical instruments	70
FINK, author	87, 96
FINNS, their Kantele	14
FINNS, their poetry	14, 48
FINNS, their songs	13
FIRMENICH, his publication	49
FISCHER, his Styrian songs	23
FLEMISH songs	24
FORSTER, his German songs	23
FRANCE, poetry of	45, 49
FRANCE, songs of	19
FRANCISQUE-MICHEL, author	19
FRANCONIA, songs of	22
FRANTISEK Martinec, his Bohemian songs	12
FULGENCE, his Cent Chants	7
GALICIA, songs of	11
GALLINI, on dancing	62
GAMLE Norske Folkviser	8
GEIJER, his Swedish songs	8
GEITLER, his Bulgarian poetry	46
GERBERT, on mediæval music	73
GERMANY, poetry of	45, 49
GERMANY, songs of	21
GIPSIES, their music	91
GNÉDITCH, on Greek songs	17
GOD save the King, tune of	35
GREECE, poetry of	45, 47, 51
GREECE, songs of	17

INDEX.   105

	PAGE		PAGE
GREEK Church music . .	68, 90	ITALY, poetry of . . .	45, 48
GREENE, his publication . .	41	ITALY, songs of	18
GROSJEAN, his Noëls . . .	64		
GRÜNBAUM, his Russian songs .	10	JAPAN, airs of	40
GRUNDTVIG, his Danish songs .	50	JAPAN, poetry of	51
GUNN, on Scotch music . .	87	JEWS, their sacred music . .	65
GUTHRIE, on Russian music .	90	JOHNSON, his Scotch songs . .	26
		JONAS, his Hebrew songs . .	68
HAEFFNER, his Swedish airs .	8	JONES, E., his publications .	7, 32
HAGEN, on the Minnesänger .	91	JONES, E., his Welsh music. .	30
HARMONY to national airs .	6, 93	JONES, J. D., his Welsh Carols .	64
HARRIES, his national hymn .	37	JONES, Sir W., on Hindu music .	81
HAUPT and Schmaler, their songs			
of the Wends	11	KALAUZ, his Servian tunes . .	13
HAXTHAUSEN, his sacred songs .	63	KÄMPEVISER, Danish . . .	8
HEBREW instruments . . .	71	KANTELE, Finnish . . .	100
HEBREW songs	65	KASTNER, on military music .	77
HELMHOLTZ, on acoustics . .	77	KAYSER, his Orpheus . . .	7
HERBERT, his Carinthian songs .	23	KHETTRA Mohana Gosvâmee, on	
HERDER, his national poetry .	44	Hindu music	81
HERZEGOVINA, poetry of . .	46	KIESEWETTER, on the music of	
HINDU music, works on . .	81	the Arabs	85
HINDUSTAN, music of . . .	39	KIESEWETTER, on the music of	
HINRICHS, on the Russian horn-		the modern Greeks . . .	89
band	90	KINLOCH, his Scotch ballads .	27
HOFFMANN von Fallersleben, his		KIRCHER, on instruments . .	76
German songs . .	22, 23, 38	KNIGHT, his Canadian airs . .	40
HOFFMANN von Fallersleben, his		KOBZA, instrument . . .	100
Polish songs	11	KOCIPINSKI, his songs of the	
HOGGS, his Jacobite Relics . .	26	Ukraine	9
HOLLAND, dances of . .	36, 56	KÖHLER, his national dances .	54
HOMMEL, his sacred songs . .	63	KOLBERG, his Polish airs . .	10
HUNGARY, poetry of . .	46, 48	KONOPKA, his songs of Cracow .	11
HUNGARY, songs of . . .	14	KORYTHO, his songs of Carniola .	13
HUSSITES, their songs. . .	12	KRETSCHMER, his songs of Ger-	
HYMNS of the Hindus . .	39	many	22
		KUHN, his songs of Switzerland .	21
ICELAND, poetry of . . .	47		
IGNAC Bognar, his Hungarian		LABORDE, on instruments . .	76
songs	15	LA Clé du Caveau . . .	20
ILLYRIA, poetry of . . .	46	LA FAGE, author	82
INDIA, music of	81	LAING, on Scotch music . .	26
INDIA, songs of	39	LA Lire Maçonne . . .	35
INDIANS, American, their music .	43	LA Morisque, dance . . .	56
INSTRUMENTS, musical . .	70	LANDSTAD, his Norwegian songs .	8
IRELAND, dances of . . .	61	LANE, on the music of Egypt .	85
IRELAND, poetry of . . .	52	LAY, on the music of China. .	95
IRELAND, songs of . . .	27	LECTURES, musical . . .	101

INDEX.

	PAGE
LE DUC, his Noëls	64
LEVEY, his Irish dances	61
LINDEMAN, his Norwegian tunes.	9
LIPINSKI, C., his songs of Galicia	11
LIPINSKI, J., his songs of Posen	11
LISENKO, on Veresai	100
LISZT, on the Gipsies	91
LITHUANIA, songs of	14
LITTLE Russia, minstrels of	100
LITTLE Russia, songs of	9, 46
LOMAN, his Dutch songs	24
LÖNNROT, his Finnish songs	14
LORRAINE, songs of	20
LUSCINIUS, on instruments	76
LWOW, on Russian songs	9
LY-KOANG-TI, Chinese author	82
LYRIC Airs, by Jones	7
MAGYARS, their songs	14
MARINER, on the songs of the Tonga Islanders	96
MARTINOWSKY, his Bohemian songs	12
MATRAY, his Hungarian songs	14
MAYER and Staab, their Hebrew songs	68
MEDIÆVAL instruments	73
MEDIÆVAL songs	91
MERSENNE, on instruments	76
MEXICO, songs of	42
MIDDLE Ages, artists of the	73
MIKLOSICH, on Slavonic poetry	91
MINNESÄNGER, mediæval	91
MINSTRELS	100
MIODUSZEWSKI, his sacred songs	64
MISSIONARIES, musical	94
MODINHAS, Portugal	18, 45
MOE, his Norwegian songs	9
MONA Melodies	32
MONTENEGRO, poetry of	46
MOORE, his Irish Melodies	28
MORAVIA, songs of	12, 48, 92
MORRIS-DANCE	56
MOSCHELES, his Tyrolese Melodies	23
MOZART, his popular tunes	23
MURPHY, his publication	55

	PAGE
MURRAY, his Roumanian songs	50
MUSICAL Curiosities, by Jones	7
NATHAN, his Hebrew Melodies	68
NATIONAL Anthem	35
NATIONAL Music, definition of the term	1
NATIONAL Music, the study of	2
NATIONAL Songs	6
NEGRO Music	41
NESSELMANN, his Lithuanian songs	14
NETHERLANDS, poetry of the	45, 47
NEW Zealanders, their music	96
NOËLS, French	64
NORSKE Fjeldmelodier	9
NORSKE Folkviser	8
NORSKE Viser	9
NORWAY, songs of	8
NYERUP, his Danish ballads	8
OFFENBACH, his Hagadah	67
ORGAN-MUSIC	57
ORPHEUS Caledonius	25
OTT, his German songs	24
OUSELEY, Sir W., on Hindu music	81
OWEN, J., his Welsh airs	32
OWEN Meredith, his Servian songs	50
PARRY, his British Harmony	29
PARRY, his Welsh melodies	30
PARRY, his Welsh tunes	28
PARSONS, his Hindu hymns	39
PAULI Zegota, his Galician songs	12
PENTATONIC scale	88
PERCY, his English poetry	34
PERDIZ, his songs of Peru	43
PERSIA, poetry of	40, 51
PERSIA, songs of	40
PERU, poetry of	45
PERU, songs of	43
PETRIE, his Irish airs	28
PLAYFORD, his Dancing Master	33
PLAYFORD, his Scotch tunes	25
POETRY, national	44

INDEX.

	PAGE
POLAND, songs of.	10
POLISH Christmas Carols	64
POLKA, dance	60
POLYNESIANS, their music	96
PONTÉCOULANT, on instruments	77
PORTUGAL, poetry of	45, 47
PORTUGAL, songs of	18
POSEN, songs of	11
PRÆTORIUS, on instruments	76
PRATCH, his Russian songs	9
PRINS, his Dutch songs	24
PRIOR, his Danish ballads	50
PROUT, on Instrumentation	77
RAHBEK, his Danish ballads	8
RAINER, the Tyrolese family	23
RALSTON, his Russian songs	50
RANZ de Vaches	21
RASMUSSEN, his Danish songs	8
RAZUMOFFSKY, on Russian Church music	90
REGALS, organs	57
REINHOLM, his Finnish songs	13
RHESA, his Lithuanian songs	14
RIBAULT de Laugardière, his Noëls	64
RICHTER, his German songs	22
RIMBAULT, his English tunes	34
RITSON, his English songs	34
RITSON, his Scotch songs	27
RITTERSBERG and Weber, their songs of Bohemia	12
RIVARÈS, his songs of Béarn	20
ROCHLITZ, author	96
ROGER, his songs of Posen	11
ROSENBERG, his Swedish tunes	8
ROUMANIA, poetry of	46, 48, 50
ROUMANIA, songs of	12
ROUMELIA, poetry of	46
RUSOF, on Veresai	100
RUSSIA, poetry of	46, 47, 50
RUSSIA, songs of	9
RUSSIAN Church music	68, 90
RUSSIAN Horn-Band	90
SABOLY, his Noëls	64
SACRED music	63
SALAMAN, his Hebrew songs	68

	PAGE
SALLABERRY, his airs of the Basques	19
SANDERS, his Greek songs	17
SANDYS, his Christmas Carols	64
SCANDINAVIAN tunes	7
SCHEFER, his Greek songs	17
SCHMID, organist, his dance-tunes	58
SCHNEIDER, on instruments	76
SCHONNER, his Tyrolese songs	23
SCHRÖTER, his Finnish songs	14
SCHUMACHER, his national hymn	38
SCOTLAND, instruments of	91
SCOTLAND, poetry of	51
SCOTLAND, songs of	24
SERVIA, poetry of	46, 48, 50
SERVIA, songs of	13
SEWARD, on the Jubilee Singers	88
SIBERIA, songs of	48
SIEBOLD, his Japanese airs	40
SIEBOLD, his Japanese instruments	78
SILBERMANN, organ-builder	59
SILCHER, his German songs	22
SILESIA, songs of	22
SLAVE songs, American	41, 88
SLAVONIC poetry	48, 91
SLAVONIC songs	9
SMIT, his Dutch songs	37
SMITH, Father	59
SOURINDRO Mohun Tagore, on Hindu music	82
SOUTH Sea Islanders, their music	96
SOWINSKI, his Polish songs	11
SPAIN, poetry of	45, 47, 50
SPAIN, songs of	18
SPAUN, his Austrian songs	23
STADLER, his songs of the Dervishes	16
STANKOVITZ, his Servian airs	13
STARTER, his Dutch songs	24
STENHOUSE, on Scotch music	26
STEVENSON, his Irish Melodies	28
ST. GEORGE, his airs of the Isle of Man	32
STYRIA, songs of	23
SULZER, his Schir Zion	65
SULZER, his Turkish music	90
SURRENNE, his Scotch dances	26

SUSHIL, his Moravian songs	12
SÜSZ, his Austrian songs	23
SVENSKA Folk-Visor	8
SVENSKA Fornsånger	8
SVENSKA Vallvisor och Hornlåtar	8
SWABODA, his Bohemian songs	12
SWEDEN, poetry of	47
SWEDEN, songs of	8
SWITZERLAND, songs of	21
SYV, his Danish ballads	8
TALVJ, on national poetry	44
TALVJ, on Slavonic poetry	91
TARENNE, his Ranz des Vaches	21
TELUGU tunes	40
THE Netherlands, poetry of	45, 47
THEORISTS, musical, oriental	86
THIBAUT, author	92
THOMAS, his Welsh songs	31
THOMPSON, his dance-tunes	56
THOMSON, G., his Scottish Airs	27
THOMSON, W., his Orpheus Caledonius	25
TIELMAN Susato, his Dutch publication	56
TONGA Islanders, their music	96
TRANSCRIPTIONS of national airs	43
TRANSYLVANIA, poetry of	46
TRAVELLERS, musical	93
TREATISES on music	81
TRINKS, his Hindu songs	39
TROUBADOURS, mediæval	92
TSCHISCHKA and Schottky, their Austrian songs	22
TUNIS, airs of	40
TURKEY, songs of	15
TYROL, songs of	23
UDVALGTE Danske Viser	8
UKRAINE, minstrel of the	100
UKRAINE, songs of the	9, 46
UNITED States, America, songs of the	40, 52
VALERIUS, his Dutch songs	24
VASHAK, his Bohemian songs	12
VEDEL, his Danish ballads	8
VENUGOPÁL Nayakkar, his Hindu tunes	40
VERDOVICH, his Bulgarian poetry	46
VERESAI, minstrel	100
VERRINDER, his Hebrew songs	68
VIEIRA, his melodies	43
VILLEMARQUÉ, his songs of Brittany	20
VILLOTEAU, on Arabic music,	38, 78, 85
VIRDUNG, on instruments	73
VOLL, organ-builder	57
VREDEMAN, his Dutch songs	24
WACHMANN, his Wallachian airs	12
WACKERBARTH, on Anglo-Saxon music	91
WACKERNAGEL, his German songs	22
WALDAU, on the dances of Bohemia	54
WALES, hornpipe of	98
WALES, songs of	28, 64
WALKER, on the Irish Bards	28
WALLACHIA, songs of	12, 90
WALLOONS, their songs	24
WEIHNACHTSLIEDER, German	63
WEINTRAUB, his Hebrew songs	66
WEITZMANN, his Greek songs	17
WEKERLIN, his French songs	19
WELCKER, on instruments	76
WENDS, their songs	11
WILLARD, on Hindu music	81
WILLEMS, his Dutch songs	24
WILLIAMS, Miss Jane, her Welsh airs	31
WILLIAMSON, his Hindu songs	39
WOJCICKI, his songs of the Crobatians, &c.	11
WOLF, his mediæval songs	91
WOLFF, A., his Hebrew songs	68
WOLFF, his Braga	7
WOLFF, his national poetry	44
WYSZ, his Swiss songs	21
YOUSSOUPOFF, on Russian sacred music	90
ZALESKI, his songs of Galicia	11
ZAMMINER, on instruments	77
ZEGOTA Pauli, his Galician songs	12

www.ingramcontent.com/pod-product-compliance
Lightning Source LLC
Chambersburg PA
CBHW031619170426
43195CB00037B/1210